COCAINE + SURFING

COCAINE + SURFING

A Sordid History of Surfing's Greatest Love Affair

CHAS SMITH

INTRODUCTION BY MATT WARSHAW

VIREO/RARE BIRD
LOS ANGELES, CALIF.

A Vireo Book | Rare Bird Books
453 South Spring Street, Suite 302
Los Angeles, CA 90013
rarebirdbooks.com

NORTH AMERICAN TRADE PAPERBACK EDITION

Simultaneously published in respective territories by Hachette Australia,
and in audio by Audible

Set in Dante
Printed in the United States

10 9 8 7 6 5 4 3 2 1

HARDCOVER ISBN: 9781945572814
PAPERBACK ISBN: 9781644280331

Publisher's Cataloging-in-Publication data
Names: Smith, Chas, author.
Title: Cocaine + Surfing : a sordid history of surfing's greatest love affair / Chas Smith.
Description: First North American Hardcover Edition | A Vireo Book |
New York, NY; Los Angeles, CA: Rare Bird Books, 2018.
Identifiers: ISBN 9781945572814
Subjects: LCSH Smith, Chas. | Surfers—Biography. | Surfing. | Cocaine. |
Cocaine abuse. | BISAC BIOGRAPHY & AUTOBIOGRAPHY / Personal
Memoirs. | BIOGRAPHY & AUTOBIOGRAPHY / Sports. |
SPORTS & RECREATION / Surfing.
Classification: LCC GV838.N65 .S65 2018 | DDC 797.32/092—dc23

For Derek Rielly

Contents

Introduction

by Matt Warshaw

Here are two things to know before diving into Chas Smith's remarkable *Cocaine and Surfing: A Love Story*.

Drugs are funny. Not always. Not often, in fact. But often enough. Like any other culturally attuned Baby Boomer, I learned this from Richard Pryor, who alchemized a raging drug habit into comic gold. Maybe you've heard of the Pryor-on-fire episode? After a five-day freebase bender in 1980, Pryor, hallucinating and hearing voices, poured a bottle of Bacardi 151 over his head, flicked his cigarette lighter, then ran flaming down his driveway and into the street. God himself was a Pryor fan, though, and Richard survived. Eighteen months later, I was in a packed movie theater for the opening weekend of Pryor's *Live on the Sunset Strip*, and there he was onscreen, earlobes all waxy and scarred, reenacting a conversation between his drug-addled self and a menacingly calm-voiced base pipe—I won't quote here; quoting Pryor never works—and while part of me knew the story was horrifying, like everybody else in the theater I was gasping and weeping and rocking back and forth with laughter.

Surfing is pointless. That's the second thing. It is joyful and gorgeous and exciting and more, absolutely, in spades, and not pointless in the nihilistic way that drugs are pointless. But pointless enough. This was hard for me to accept. At age nine, riding waves became the maypole of my life, and everything else—school, career, travel, family, friends, love interests—would trail behind like so many fluttering ribbons. Surfing first, the rest second or third or whatever. I did that for forty years. For a long time, it felt noble and serious and superior. Eventually I got married and had a son, demoted surfing to its rightful place below family, friends, career, and came to believe that surfing was simply a way of pleasuring yourself. A beautiful thing to do, healthy and compelling and of a far higher order of pleasure than what all of us think of when the phrase "pleasuring yourself" is used. I would argue in fact that surfing is indeed "a most supreme pleasure," as Captain Cook (or his ghostwriter) put it centuries ago. I would go even further and say that surfing is to sports-world pleasure what Richard Pryor is to comedy.

Isn't that enough? For a totally nonproductive act of self-pleasure, isn't it enough that it be a *very good* type of self-pleasure, maybe the best of all? Apparently not. We want more. We want significance and weight.

And thus a tendency for the long-form examination of surfing (and many short-form takes as well) to overreach. To burden the sport with importance, to pair it thematically with all manner of greater meaning, up to and including enlightenment. A filmmaker called me last week to pitch a multi-part documentary series on surfing that would provide viewers with (his words) "a holistic examination of the human condition past, present, and future through the lens of international surf culture." I don't speak for all surfers. But my experience, and the experience of pretty much everyone I've surfed with over the past fifty wonderful wave-filled years, is that we're not doing anything constructive, much less enlightening, out there. We are mostly practicing. Because, wow, this is a hard sport. We are trying to do it right for just a few seconds in a row. We unwind a little afterward, if things go well. But just as often, we end up frustrated, sometimes horribly so. Because, and I mean *seriously*, it is a really fuck-off hard sport.

I would devour a book on surfing and frustration with the same single-mindedness I give to avoiding books on surfing and enlightenment.

But for now we have *Cocaine and Surfing*, which, now that I think about it, is actually a much better fit, book-wise, than frustration and surfing.

Nobody but Chas Smith could have pulled off *Cocaine and Surfing*. His comedic chops, for starters, are unequaled in the world of surf, and not just in 2018, but for all time. More importantly, he understands, to the finest degree, that drugs are horrible but funny and surfing is amazing but pointless. Which makes *Cocaine and Surfing* a high-wire act. Comedy leads, but other, darker elements are present at all times. There are shadows behind the laughter. You get that from the opening pages, as two nameless, gacked-out pro surfers wrestle in Chas's car while he chauffeurs them to a club in Huntington Beach, half amused and half pissed off. It is a three-page comic riff, but with an aftertaste of sadness, as you realize that both surfers are destined for a ten-year hangover, and very likely a depressed middle age. Hilarity cut with pain and sadness and anger. It's a hard mix to get right. Incredibly hard. You bring Pryor-grade skills to the table when you sit down and write a book like this, in other words, or you burn the first draft and go back to bitchy three-paragraph blog posts about world tour judging system.

Back to the anger for a moment, because anger is the secret power of *Cocaine and Surfing*, as it is for nearly all of Chas Smith's work. The sport may be amazing and pointless to him, but it is also dear, and personal in the way that all obsessions are personal. Something worth protecting. Chas watches as our once-undomesticated sport is yoked and dragged from the cultural outback to a bland common area filled with committee-designed surfwear and bloodless journalism and drone-like pros who, after a close loss, rather than impaling their boards on the nearest fence post and storming off the beach, smile gamely into the camera and say their opponent surfed great, that it's all a learning experience, that they're looking forward to the next event. All of this makes Chas angry. The blandness, yes. But mostly the hypocrisy. The sports own self-betrayal. We should know better— we *used* to know better—than to try and reshape surfing into a sport that fits into a Mutual of Omaha ad campaign, or an Olympic telecast. Selling the sport isn't a crime. But sell it on our own terms, the way Bruce Brown did with *Endless Summer*. Make them come to us. And if they don't, so what? But no, we continue slicing off our legacy of cool, of independence, piece by piece, in exchange for a seat in the nosebleed section of mainstream culture. Then we compound the error (not "we," actually, but the World Surf League, the NYSE-traded surfwear companies, and whoever convinced the IOC to make surfing an Olympic sport for the 2020 games in Tokyo) by passing off this auto-swindle as growth and progress.

That's where Chas's anger comes from. And if you follow his work—mostly on the BeachGrit website, but also in his excellent first book *Welcome to Paradise, Now Go To Hell*—you already know the glory of an angry Chas Smith: the dandified scarecrow in worn Louis Vuitton drivers and a flawless Dior shirt, pirouetting his way across beaches and boardrooms and party halls in a weaponized good mood, encouraging us to laugh both at him and with him as he delivers one loafer-shod kick after the other to the sternum of any person or entity who would further chip away at whatever free-range soul surfing has left.

In other words, for all the comedy and pointlessness I've talked about here vis-à-vis drugs and surf, and *Cocaine and Surfing*, there are stakes on the table. There are risks involved. For drug users, of course. But drug use can be temporary. Reversals are possible. Today's bent coke-out surfer might be straight and redeemed tomorrow. The stakes for surfing, however, in terms of its identity—the way the sport presents and views itself—are also high, but not reversible. Barring some kind of apocalyptic global socio-industrial meltdown, a fully tamed and enfranchised and corporate-friendly version of surfing will never gain back what it lost.

Do I think this book will halt, or even slow, our slide into a broader, safer, blander age?

No. I do not. But *Cocaine and Surfing* is truthful and smart and very very funny, and when I laugh it hurts less.

Prologue

It is cold outside, and gray. Heavy-sweater weather. Maybe even thin down-filled-jacket-paired-with-stocking-cap weather and it smells like cow. Like manure, wet feed, and sour milk, which only makes sense since we are in Lemoore, California, the official "Home of Cows, More Cows, and Chas Smith's Damned Ex-Wife."

Just kidding. My damned ex-wife is from neighboring Visalia, but all of inland central California is basically the same thing and a place I swore I'd never return. Then Kelly Slater went and created the perfect wave here.

Yes, the world's most celebrated surfer decided, as he neared retirement, to shake a tanned fist at God and man-make a legitimately perfect wave using some patented plow in what used to be a water-ski lake in what used to be my damned ex-wife's general neighborhood some hundred miles away from the ocean, all cow-stinky and gray.

A wave that barrels properly. That drives down the length of the green lake and barrels perfectly every single time. Nothing like this has ever been done. Previous wave pools create a surf that dribbles along in an embarrassing, weak, low-energy kind of way. Kelly's wave pool fires the imagination. Even surfers who travel the world riding the ocean's best waves are clamoring for an invite.

"Surf Ranch" is what they are calling it, and it is the jewel in the World Surf League's crown. Surfing as a "sport" has always been hampered by nature. By God. Sometimes waves show up. Sometimes they don't. And how is a sporting event supposed to be held in such randomness? The football field doesn't change and neither does the basketball court, so the World Surf League purchased the Surf Ranch property and its patented plow technology from Kelly Slater in order to equalize the arena. To make surfing a proper sport. And so the new World Surf League CEO invited me and twelve crusty surf journalists and surf photographers up to surf it and witness the future.

She is trying to understand what we are, God bless her, trying to figure out what makes our hearts beat. The last CEO, Mr. Paul Speaker, came from the National Football League and I thought he was a dipshit. He refused each of my impassioned pleas for an interview, so I made fun of him every day in the surf media until he vacated the position. The new CEO, Ms. Sophie Goldschmidt, came from the Women's National Basketball Association and seems to be taking an honest shot at knowing what this is all about, and so here I am in the cold and gray and stink listening to her give us all a warm introduction.

"I'm so glad you could all be with us here today," she says in a proper British accent. "Everyone is going to have so much fun, I trust, and this safety briefing will ensure just that. We are very proud of what we've built." She is tall, pretty, with eyes that look too innocent for all of this and a smile that looks too pure and I don't know if I will be able to muster the internal strength to make fun of her every day. "Before we begin, though, I think it is only right to recognize that today is the day Andy Irons passed away."

The room is silent.

"I never had the privilege of meeting him, though I know many of you knew him very well, and as I learn about surfing's history, it is clear what an impact he had." Eleven of the twelve crusty surf journalists and surf photographers keep their eyes down. I look sideways at my best Australian pal/biz partner who looks like he is in a bad spot, having had four or maybe six too many whiskey sodas the previous night. She clears her throat after what feels too long. "And now allow me to introduce you to our head of water safety…"

The head of water safety is a handsome man who tells us not to screw around, but I'm thinking about Andy Irons and not the dislocated shoulder I'm going to get in two hours by screwing around.

Andy Irons.

The three-time champ from Hawaii died November 2, 2010, alone in a Dallas hotel room from what the county's medical office concluded was cardiac arrest due to a severe blockage of a heart artery and acute mixed-drug ingestion including Xanax, methadone, and metabolites of cocaine. He was thirty-two years old.

The causes of his death surprised no one in this cloistered world. Every crusty surf journalist and surf photographer in this room had either gone big with him, cocaine everywhere, dusting everything, or caught him in full pin-pricked pupil, incessant prattle mode. He was a giant character but also not an outlier, and while his death was an utter tragedy, it was not necessarily a shock.

Drugs and surfing, especially cocaine, felt synonymous with professional surfing those eight-odd years ago. It still does. It's always snowing in Orange County, or so they say, and I look at Sophie. She is listening intently to the head of water safety at a perfect man-made wave, trying to turn this professional surfing into a proper sport while also respecting its past, God bless her, but as long as I'm around, that ain't happening. Surfing, at its core, is an unruly, fouled, smutty disaster. Its past littered with felons, smugglers, addicts, narcissists, and creeps. Its present defined by crusty surf journalists and surf photographers. Its future a certain disaster—but it is our disaster.

Our glorious disaster.

1

The Call to Adventure!

I can smell the saltwater rot each time the shoe bounces off of my temple, each time it grinds into my cheek. And it must be a Volcom Creedler because its owner is a professional surfer sponsored by the surf brand Volcom and has been forever, but I don't have the luxury of looking over and finding out because I have to concentrate on driving in a straight-ish line.

"Don't fucking say anything! Don't fucking tell him anything!" The kicks are now accompanied by shouting. "Don't fucking…" and then giggling and then more shouting. "He'll fucking write about it! He's a fucking surf…journalist!"

As the shoe retreats for a moment, I sigh, readjust the rearview mirror, and study the gyrating ball wedged up against a car seat in the back seat of my Volkswagen Jetta Wagon. The professional surfer is wearing a black sweatshirt featuring Volcom's new tagline "Live For This" and I see it getting ripped while his tan arms try to protect his ribs from a barrage of jabbing, pulling fists. Bushy hair everywhere.

"Don't…fucking…surf…journalist!"

To be honest, I'm amazed that this particular surfer is still sponsored at all. Volcom sold to French multinational Kering a few years ago for $600 million and by many accounts is not performing up to expectations. The luxury group hoped to position it next to its other brands, Saint Laurent, Gucci, Balenciaga, and McQueen—except Volcom's old tagline was "Youth Against Establishment" and a signature product is a T-shirt featuring an owl over the words "Hoo farted?" Sales are lagging behind expectations, and brand managers, team managers, executive vice presidents, and professional surfers are getting cut in a Reign of Terror. These troubles are not unique to Volcom. Across the surf industry bros are getting let go and executives with gilded resumes from Disney and the NFL swoop in to take their spots and make things right, but things only get more conservative. More buttoned up. Tighter. The look and feel of ExxonMobil. A true apocalypse.

Or maybe the youth just aren't against the establishment these days. Maybe they're cool with it. Maybe they live for something else. Not this. Or maybe it is just a little too transparently antiestablishment to be part of a giant French multinational that changed its name from PPR to Kering because it sounds like "caring." Whatever the case, it was Kering's initial investment that allowed Volcom to make its first closed-toe shoe, the Creedler, a misguided attempt at replicating the Vans Classic which failed beyond badly because nobody can replicate the Vans Classic, not even Saint Laurent.

"Fucking! Surf! Journalist!"

The guy shouting is also a professional surfer, except sponsored by Reef. He has pinned Volcom completely now and might be pinching his nipples. Or twisting them. Reef is owned by VF Corp, which also coincidentally owns Vans. Reef is tailspinning almost as bad as Volcom, but the brand's sponsored surfer is doing well—at least right now in this particular physical exchange. Wailing, jabbing, pulling, ripping. Screaming. Angry. Winning in a mixed martial arts style I would not have thought him capable of.

I wonder if he is wearing a pair of Reef's Mick Fanning signature beer bottle opening sandals? Yes, Reef literally and honestly makes a sandal with a bottle-opener on the bottom. Like, you walk down the street on your way to a friend's BBQ, walk through dog urine or bum urine or horse urine—depending, I suppose, on where your friend lives— then get to his house, go to his backyard, open his cooler, grab a beer, take your sandal off and use its bottom to pop the cap. Literally. Honestly. But I can't see from my angle if he is wearing them or not, and the two keep shifting and squirming, gyrating, and the anger level seems to be rising.

"...FUCK...DON'T...FUCKING...SURF...JOURNALIST!"

And then it hits another level. I think Reef is jamming his hand into Volcom's mouth while twisting his nipples. I think he is trying to remove teeth or a tongue. I am going to whip around and say, "Knock it off you two! I'm driving here!" but I don't know how to deliver the line without sounding ridiculously paternal, especially in a station wagon featuring a baby car seat, so I accept the abuse. Plus, I'm getting a little curious about this story that is so secret it is causing one grown professional surfer in the twilight of his career to smash another, also in the twilight of his career, in the back seat of a soccer mom car.

The Creedler—it's totally a Creedler, I can see it now with its misshapen toe and too-high rise—brushes past my nose and then slams into my eye and I swerve, almost crossing into oncoming traffic. The kicking stops along with the shouting. In my rearview mirror, the fighters are adjusting themselves—maybe scared straight, maybe calming down.

But then the giggling starts up again. "...so his dad..." I glance back in the rearview. Reef is sitting sullenly, arms crossed over the words on his sweatshirt that reads "Just Passing Through," which is that brand's tagline, looking out the window and apparently accepting his fate. I again try to see if he is wearing the beer sandal, but his feet are down in the dark spaces. In the dark spaces I get in trouble for never cleaning and which usually have crushed-up banana bits and gluten-free pretzels and sometimes organic preschool art projects floating about. I hope he is wearing the Mick Fanning signature sandal so bad. He'll have a real treat when he opens his next beer.

Volcom is sitting upright and trying to get it all out between fits of glee but still in a protective hunch, waiting for the pain to potentially start again. In the traditional pose of youth against establishment.

"...his old mate was out walking with one of his friends in the bush near Blueys, right? They were near Blueys?" He looks over at Reef who is not about to provide help, but then Volcom doesn't need it because remembers suddenly. "It was Blueys, because they have all those koala crossings in the trees over the road there! So the two of them were walking together and the friend asked him if he knew that koalas were getting STDs and heaps of them were dying. And old mate didn't believe him at first but he kept going on and on saying shit like, 'Yeah it's chlamydia and heaps of them are dying but the worst part is that the drop bears are getting it now too.' And old mate said he didn't believe it but later that day was caught out at the pub with…" and he is having difficulty containing himself. "With…a…dinger on his head!"

He is laughing so hard now that his spasms are shaking the car while Reef angrily yells, "Fuck you! Fuck you! HE'S going to fucking write about it now! Thanks!" and not in a funny joking way either, leaving me to really wonder how in the hell either of them thought this story would possibly be interesting to anyone, especially an American. It is only by the grace of God, and enough time spent living in Australia, that I can piece together the narrative by half-understanding the pertinent bits. "Drop bears" are a regional folklore. I think maybe carnivorous koalas that drop from the trees onto unsuspecting heads and eat them? Or turn them into koala zombies? Like chupacabras, maybe. Something like that. A "dinger" I know for sure is regional slang for condom. Or maybe for sure. Australian slang moves faster than greased lightning. Blueys I've got. It is a sandbar wedge somewhere near Newcastle. Or maybe it's that river mouth closer to Coolangatta.

In fairness, I suppose the story has its moments, but it is not the sort that could be written without many explanatory segues and I still don't see how it would reflect poorly on anyone but the father and mostly, who in their right mind would care?

A wave of depression washes over me.

This.

This kicking, this pointlessness, this wildly oversensitive guarding of even the most ludicrous information, drop bears and STDs, is my lot in life because Reef is right. I am a surf journalist. A fucking surf journalist. And it wasn't supposed to be this way. I was supposed to have waved goodbye to this shallow end of the swimming pool years ago. I was supposed to be a Pulitzer Prize-winning war reporter by now, spilling valuable words on the plight of Syrian refugees while dodging bullets. Or maybe in the White House briefing room being shouted down by the press secretary for speaking truth to power. Or front row at the Fendi show in Paris, across from Anna Wintour, noting that the monster collection pairs playful and classic in a delightfully Lagerfeldian way. Or writing a coming-of-age novel set in Palm Springs during the White Party. Or scribbling my third *New Yorker* story of the year about the joys of fatherhood and winning yet another Pulitzer. Or anywhere but here.

Thankfully we arrive at our destination, the godforsaken Shorebreak Hotel in Huntington Beach, pausing my tortured reflection. Or almost pausing it. How does a surf journalist look at sixty? Does he look like an asshole? Does he just completely cave and wear the Reef Mick Fanning beer-opening sandal? Is drinking urine his penance for hanging on to a young man's game way too long?

I park four blocks away in the first space I see, under a strange fat pine, and am happy to leave but no one seems in a hurry. Volcom is still giggling. Reef is digging in his pants pocket. And then he pulls an inch-by-inch Ziploc baggie. And then he is dumping white powder on the Jetta's center console, organizing it into three straight lines. And then he is rolling up a dollar bill. He sniffs the first up his nose in one quick snort, hands the dollar bill to his erstwhile Volcom antagonist and the sniff is repeated, and then up to me.

"Thanks for driving, mate." Reef is now happy. I put on my fake cheer and say, "No worries. Glad you found me…" while handing the dollar bill back to him.

"Go for it, mate, it's yours," he says, nodding to the lonely line.

"I'm good," I say.

He shrugs, bends over, and takes care of what's left, then brushes the console off, rubs his finger across his gums, and opens his door.

Minutes ago he was smashing the shit out of his friend so some non sequitur weirdness could stay hidden from a "surf journalist." Now he has just finished smashing a good bit of blow—and dried apple juice, kid dirt from an "organic preschool," and God only knows what else—without even pausing.

It was kind that he offered some up, though. Australians, even the complete derelicts, are usually generous. When I was very young, my family took a camping trip down the California coast and in the redwoods we ran into some Australians who had locked their keys in their car. They stood outside of it very frustrated, not knowing what to do.

My dad, having insisted on only ever owning old and perpetually broken cars, quickly fashioned a small hook out of a hanger, fished it down their door, and popped their locks. They were so grateful that they gave him a giant can of Fosters. He took it, thanked them, and we got back on the road.

I sat in the back seat leaning over and staring at that can of beer. They had pronounced it "bee."

"Thanks for your help, mate. Here, take a bee…"

And I couldn't believe my dad had taken it. I had never ever seen him with alcohol in his hand. I had never seen him drink and as far as I knew he never had. We were Christians and Christians didn't drink, smoke, swear, or gamble. But there the Fosters sat next to him on the bench seat of our 1981 Ford Econoline. Big, glistening, still cold. It represented all the sin in the entire world to me. All of hell's hot fire.

At the next gas stop, he threw it away. I asked him why he had taken it, why hadn't he told them that he didn't drink beer because we were Christians? He told me that they were just being friendly with what they had and it was rude to turn people down to their faces when they didn't know any better.

And look at me all these years later, not following in my father's footsteps. Being totally rude to two Australians who definitely don't know any better. Then again, my dad had never gotten between Australian surfers and their cocaine. Or any surfers and their cocaine, for that matter. It is cherished far more than beer. Far more than maybe anything except surfing. The two pursuits have become more or less synonymous. Cocaine and surfing, surfing and cocaine. So synonymous, in fact, that the thought I'll write about lines being done off of my center console doesn't even register as a potential liability—unlike the possibility of STDs being passed on to the unsuspecting via mythical koalas, which had created spasms of rage.

Reef swings the back door open and is followed by Volcom, and then I follow too because I'm depressed about my urine-drinking future and need to drown my sorrows in something proper—or at least proper while I'm still almost young.

We walk four blocks under palms and a tree that smells like semen, past Dr. Ding surfboard repair, past Chuck Dent surfboards, past an off-brand acai bowl place, past North Shore Poke Co., and to the Shorebreak: a monument to bad taste featuring a font not even a first-year design student would find appropriate. A colorway that screams "What?" A restaurant named Zimzala that is getting changed into a restaurant named Pacific Hideaway, but nobody knows that yet.

We walk up the stairs, past giant portraits of professional surfer stars that look like they were shot in a studio at Sears, to the packed "bar." Even though the surf industry apocalypse, the unrelenting Reign of Terror. Everyone here is going to get fired tomorrow. Probably. Still, sweat is dripping from the ceiling down the walls. The surf industry still enjoys partying like it's 1991. I don't think it knows any other way.

People are yelling loud nothings into each other's ears with clenched jaws. Beer is being bought but not consumed, just swung around by its neck and spilled onto an impossibly sticky floor. The Sears surf stars are staring down from the walls. They know how this feels, and they aren't judging.

A highlight reel of some damned surf contest that happened six years ago in Portugal plays on the overhead televisions. The bathroom line stretches through Zimzala. Pinpricked pupils and sweat and jaw muscles. Some terrible reggae plays over the sound system. And a six-year-old Portugal contest. And conspiracies and loud, loud conversations yelled into ears and wiping noses and rubbing noses and jittery movements and much blinking and attempts at dancing except how can reggae be danced to in any era?

I know way too many people here. I know almost all of them, and I should not be here. I should be in Damascus or Washington, DC or Paris or Stockholm accepting my Pulitzer. Or, probably not Pulitzer, if I am going to look at my talent level honestly, but what is the Golden Globes for writing? I should not be a surf journalist, in any case, and my depression is as encompassing as a Balenciaga blizzard wool-blend sweater. As enveloping as it must be for the Kering executive who had the brilliant idea to buy the surf brand Volcom for $600 million.

"Kering, ha…" I think to myself as a pair of too-serious-for-the-moment board short designers race past mumbling something about the genius of Joseph, or maybe Thomas, Campbell. I bet high fashion thinks it has surfing beat with regards to cocaine. I bet Saint Laurent and Gucci and Balenciaga and McQueen each feel they have done them some cocaine. That they know cocaine. That they're intimates. That they have lived that cocaine life. But I once became a male model to impress my wife and got to see the way that fashion thinks about and uses cocaine. It's all right, I guess. They've done a pretty good job, but they're also fickle. Same with music, art, finance, politics, real proper sports, and the culinary industry. Sometimes cocaine is in vogue and that's what everyone is doing, but then it falls out of style and the restaurateurs get onto meth, the artists get onto an acid revival, the musicians get into MDMA, the politicians find PCP, the real proper sportsmen get some HGH and weed, and the financiers crush up low-dose naltrexone and smoke it while the models indulge in bath salts.

Surfing's flame for cocaine has never dimmed. Has never even flickered. She has loved her cocaine virtuously, decorously, passionately, almost monogamously, since as long as I've been around. And I rack my brain, while the surf industry jitters around me, trying to imagine two things more inextricably enmeshed.

Vlad Putin and sick judo skills? No. While it certainly feels like a hot affair, those two have only canoodled since 1960.

Donald J. Trump and hyperbole? A long time, yes, but the man also sometimes dallies with vicious understatement.

Gay men and moustaches? A beautiful relationship, to be sure, and maybe ancient, but not even close to monogamous.

Surfing and cocaine are rare, like elderly semi-perverse grandparents who have been married forever yet still can't keep their hands off each other. The room smells like 1991 and is packed with surfers necking beers but not drinking and trying to dance and talking loudly and rubbing noses vigorously while solving the world's problems even though they are very paranoid that the world is out to get them, and I wonder if this is why I am still a surf journalist. That God wants me to share a bizarre love story. A love story loftier than anything William Shakespeare ever wrote, or at least longer lasting. A love story with more heat than any Ryan Gosling has ever been in, including *The Notebook*. A love story that both sickens the stomach and soars the heart.

Could it be?

Is this my special purpose? What I was born to do? What I've been searching for?

Cocaine?

2

Refusal of the Call!

No. I feel a surge of existential disgust and push through the paranoia and reggae and Sears portraits. Past some big-wave surfer who is rumored to be a swinger, run down the stairs and through the doors out onto Fifth Street. The air feels hot. Heavy. Manufactured, but that has more to do with this part of Huntington Beach's 2009 faux-urban vibe. I can't breathe, I can't fucking breathe, and I tug on my Turbonegro poly-cotton-blend sweater trying to assist oxygen through my neck and into my lungs but then become self-conscious when I remember I haven't been surfing in two weeks and so my wetsuit neck tan has faded entirely away. If any surf industry bros catch me out here without a neck tan, I'll be doomed. They'll tell everyone I haven't been surfing in at least two weeks, or maybe even longer, and my house of cards will collapse, so I leave my sweater alone and let it cover my shame.

But it is so hot and I'm walking fast and getting hotter, skinny palm trees swaying against an iconic orange night sky overhead. A lone seagull bellows somewhere down by the pier. I should have run up the street and found my car under its fat pine and driven anywhere, driven home, but I didn't. And now I'm walking aimlessly down the PCH before turning up Main Street, eyes down, refraining from tugging on my sweater, just trying to breathe. Passing Jack's Surf Shop. Passing Perqs Nightclub and wondering if I should duck into another bar to order double vodkas and calm down. But I can't risk running into any more surf industry bros—not in this state, anyhow—not with this lack of wetsuit neck tan, so I keep walking.

And do you remember what you wanted to be when you grew up? Was it something that would have benefited the greater good? An artist? A dancer? A teacher, poet, fireman, superhero? President? Prime Minister? Astronaut? Did you become it? Are you happy? Are you benefiting the greater good?

Nobody dreams of becoming a surf journalist. I fantasized about being a marine biologist when I was eight years old, before it became clear to everyone, including me, that I was not mentally equipped to deal with observable facts and shit. But then it did become clear and I shifted toward wanting to become a Stinger missile-smuggling "medical missionary" like my Uncle Dave. I studied in Egypt, traveled in Syria, Yemen, Somalia, and Azerbaijan with two fabulous coconspirators, learned enough Arabic to sound like an asshole. I never got to smuggle Stinger missiles but had some fine adventures right as the world tumbled headlong into The Age of Radical Islam. I wrote about some of them for magazines, like about grime music in Somalia and "How to Run from Al-Qaeda on a 150cc Motorcycle in the Marib" and decided that I was a great new journalist. I was the second coming of Norman Mailer, except whoever the Golden Globes version is. And then Israel invaded Lebanon and there I went, ending up in a Hezbollah dungeon. At that moment I cursed my fate, my recklessness, and begged God for a way out. Any way out.

He answered my prayers and took me away from the Hezbollah dungeon and the bizarre interrogator who kept insisting that Jennie Garth from *Beverly Hills 90210* was super cute. Away from radical Islam and war and missiles. He took me to surf, and I breathed a sigh of relief thinking, "Whew," and "Jennie Garth is okay but not super cute," though I totally admitted to the bizarre interrogator that she was hotter than Beyoncé.

The things a man will do to save his fingernails.

A honking horn startles me into the present. It's an older model Toyota Camry with two surfboards strapped to the top, fins down, cruising very slowly down Main Street. Clearly from Chino or Riverside.

Nobody who knows ever puts a board on a car with its fins down. I've sat through raging, multiple-hours-long debates over whether it is better to put fins forward or to put fins back but never ever *ever* down. It is one of the infinite ways to be a kook.

Surfers are a strange breed in this way. The amount of sub-contextual notes and cues, the number of dos and don'ts—mostly don'ts—is staggering. Knee-buckling. Don't walk down the beach with your leash attached to your leg. Don't hype a hurricane swell. Don't paddle out with more than two friends. Don't claim a turn. Don't exaggerate wave height. Do wildly undersell wave height. Don't wear a neoprene surf hat. Don't wear anything except a black wetsuit in the water. Don't ever wear a spring suit. Ever. Don't talk in the lineup. Keep your hands in your armpits in the lineup. Don't keep your hands in your armpits in the lineup if another surfer already has his hands in his armpits. Don't rub sand in your wax before paddling out. Sometimes rub sand in your wax before paddling out depending on thirty distinct factors. Don't surf with a buckled knee because then everyone will think you are trying to copy professional surfer Craig Anderson and nothing could be more transparently try-hard in the moment than trying to copy professional surfer Craig Anderson. Don't try hard.

Etcetera, ad infinitum.

There are more unwritten rules than there are Hindu gods and the sum of these subtleties, utterly devoid of any real value, is what makes up the surfer's mind. He is so oppressively shallow because his mind is stuttering over things like this, over where to put his hands in the lineup, how to put his boards on his car.

If his neck tan is as delineated as it should be.

God took me from the Hezbollah dungeon to surf, anyhow, and at first I breathed a giant sigh of relief and thought, "I'll kick here until the dust settles." I had always loved surfing and it felt wonderful to follow the professional surf tour to perfectly non-dangerous France, Australia, and Tahiti. To write about beaches and sun and waves. I was living the life and after a few years, my batteries were sufficiently charged. It was time to go back to war.

I figured my way out was to write a surf book where I burned all my bridges, and so I wrote one about Oahu's North Shore. A place no surf industry person really talks about publically because it is violent and filled with scary people. Slaps, cracks, choke-outs, Spam, false cracks, and knocks on da head. The surf industry person doesn't like any of these things and will generally shy away from direct conflict if he can, preferring to passive-aggressively avoid his enemy. But he also has to go to the North Shore every winter where passive-aggressive avoidance doesn't work, and he doesn't want to get smashed for anything that could be misinterpreted as disrespectful and so he spends a month each year with his eyes darting, his mouth shut and scared.

If I wrote a book about it, I'd be committing surf industry seppuku and become an untouchable corpse. *Welcome to Paradise, Now Go to Hell* was supposed to be a complete disembowelment. It was supposed to get surfing's living nightmare furious with me. Somehow, though, surfing's living nightmare liked it. Or maybe liked it.

Eddie "Fast Eddie" Rothman, the man who runs the North Shore like a scarred knuckle don, was the book's star and couldn't be dreamt up by even the most ludicrous imagination. He is compact, powerful, tough, with a voice like thunder and a grip like pain. He is also somehow Jewish and from Philadelphia. When he walks into a room, the surf industry person begins shaking and quietly praying that Fast Eddie will go talk to someone else. Anyone else.

I spent time with him, yeah, but he was angry with me before the book came out, maybe anticipating an unfair portrayal. He called me and gave me an earful of hell and I thought, "Good. No more surf for sure." But he called me again six months after it came out and chuckled his low, guttural chuckle. "You know. You write fuckin' good. It's a funny book."

Son of a bitch. Thanks, Eddie. Thanks a lot.

It was also supposed to get the surf industry, so staid and conservative, to toss me out on my ear for telling too many secrets and making fun of too many surf industry executives. I wrote gleefully about how one executive from Billabong, the largest surf company at the time, was slapped by Fast Eddie and how he deserved it. That

Billabong executive later became a major part of the professional surf tour, now called the World Surf League, and I thought, "So long!" but I *still* wasn't tossed out. I was simply passive-aggressively avoided and whispered about and generally not liked by everyone in the World Surf League except its senior vice president of global identity.

I toyed around with the non-surf epics I would write. Infiltrating gangs that deal in black market food, tentatively titled, in my mind, *Tonight, We Dine in Hell*. Or infiltrating American separatist groups, tentatively titled *Reports From Hell Before Breakfast*. Or sailing a boat from Yemen to Egypt around a Saudi blockade tentatively titled *Aljahim* ("hell" in Arabic). They were my destiny, what I was meant to do, but I couldn't get any internal traction on the topics. I'd feel inspired and then the inspiration would get mashed beneath shit-stirring and surfing and so I slunk back to surf journalism to pen such instant classics as "Advice: Self-motivation is overrated!" and "How to: Change without a towel!" trying to find some sort of meaning where no meaning exists. Fucking surfers. Fucking surf journalism. Fucking below-the-knee surf trunks.

I walk past the Billabong store and see they've debuted a collection featuring Andy Warhol's art on surf trunks and T-shirts. A giant cardboard printout in the window features his quote, "I came out of the womb on a surfboard." Did he really say that? What is it even supposed to mean? Andy Warhol never had a neck tan and for sure never surfed.

Pop culture's dance with surfing is always a funny thing. I suppose if surfers had any sort of understandable depth, or any depth full stop, then Hollywood would have pounced on them as archetypes and figured out long ago how to capture the specifics enough to make a surf blockbuster, but have you seen Hollywood's surf films? Have you seen *Chasing Mavericks* or *Blue Crush* or *Point Break* (either of them) or *North Shore* or *Big Wednesday* or *The Perfect Wave* or *Soul Surfer* or *In God's Hands*?

The best of them are laughably bad. The worst, a forgettable cringe.

Hollywood can't get the surfer even halfway right and I think it's a proximity issue. Many in Hollywood, many directors and producers and actors, think they surf. Their glittering town perched on the Pacific causes them to believe they know what it all means because they walk out of Malibu homes, grab a goofy yellowed seven-foot pintail, and go sit in the puddle out front. But surfing and belonging to surf are two entirely separate things. Belonging to surf, in my definition, is to be part of the surf industrial complex. Those who either work for a surf brand in some capacity as a photographer, writer, shaper, or who have at some point in their lives. Those who have so oriented their lives around surf that they watch World Surf League events while chatting about professional surfer form on message boards. Those whose productivity slowly drains away because they surf instead of working. Those who have pterygium.

And that is exactly what Hollywood is missing as it relates to the surfer. Pterygium, also called "surfer's eye." What WebMD describes as "a growth of pink, fleshy tissue on the conjunctiva, the clear tissue that lines your eyelids and covers your eyeball. It usually forms on the side closest to your nose and grows toward the pupil area."

Quite basically, pterygia are scales. Scales that begin growing over the eye because surfers sit out in the water long enough thinking about where to put their hands and so God, in His transcendence, knows that they will go blind and puts scales over their eyes to protect them from the sun's fiery wrath as it bounces off the water. They don't generally cause blindness, but they cause blurriness of vision.

Surfers have scales covering their eyes. I have never met a director or producer with scales covering his and I have only met one actor who might be close to having them—Jimmy Caan's boy, Scott. But almost every real surfer, every professional surfer or surf brand manager or executive vice president to the bros, has either full-blown pterygium or the beginnings of pterygium, or bones covering the inside of his ears, also known as "surfer's ear." He has chosen surfing over clear eyesight or over hearing. Sometimes over both. Scott Caan went one better, too. He chose to star in the remake of *Hawaii Five-0*, just so he could surf.

My own baby pterygia make me look stoned all the time. I don't smoke weed.

Surfing truly is a wild obsession that must have begun in a place so fantastic that the surfer's reptilian brain was seared forever with its preeminence. A place more glorious than human vision can contain, thus making it redundant. A place where palm trees sway in warm trade breezes and the water is not cold and the waves are plentiful and iconic and perfect. Surfing must have begun in Hawaii, where Scott Caan actively shoots his career in the foot. A tropical paradise floating proud in the blue Pacific. Islands of frangipani and hula and aloha and mahalo. Islands of Pipeline and Waimea and Pupukea and Peahi and Hanalei. Islands of surf. A dream better than eyesight, hearing, or proper acting work. Right?

Surf and Hawaii do make sense together. They belong together, and it feels as if the fiftieth state birthed the wave sliding onto the world. But did you know that surfing came to Hawaii, along with hula and coconuts and gods and goddesses, from Tahiti? It was on those towering, craggy, postcard-y, equally gorgeous green folds that Polynesian power consolidated then moved outward.

The ancient Polynesians never figured out how to write language or make a wheel or dig metals from the ground, but they could sail like no people had sailed before or, likely, will ever sail again. With neither map nor compass they would push off into the vast Pacific, discover new islands, populate them, plant coconuts, sacrifice people by crushing their bones, and make their way back home again.

The ocean was their world and they would sail by constellation, by cloud pattern, by current, by smell. And the first European explorers to travel the Micronesian and Polynesian Islands could not believe these primitives could sail so well. It was a popular belief at the time that God simply planted them on their islands. Later, when science replaced God as the *du jour* belief system, the world's foremost thinkers assumed Polynesia's islands were the remains of sunken continents and the inhabitants were the sad detritus of once great civilizations. All the way until the 1960s, scholars were confused as to how islanders go to their islands. Their methods were simply too rudimentary to be able to navigate the great Pacific, and their boats too shitty.

Human navigation, even at its most European-sophisticated, is a total junk show when compared to that of other animals. We don't read magnetic fields or innately know true north. We can't follow multigenerational, multi-thousand-mile travel patterns like the Monarch butterfly. We can't even count our steps and dead reckon like the Sahara Desert ant, or at least not without a Fitbit.

But the ancient Micronesians and Polynesians, the Pacific Islanders, were good enough to make the animal kingdom blush and to make the sophisticated European seem like the backward cave dweller that he is. They were not subpar at all. They were magnificent.

The Marshall Islanders, to the north and west of Tahiti, had a system, for example. There are five main islands and twenty-nine atolls occupying some seventy square miles, and they were completely isolated from each other and from any other bigger land mass. Over the millennia, they established a system called "wave piloting" in order to get around with an almost inhuman sense, and it almost disappeared from the face of the earth because we decided to test our gorgeous hydrogen bombs there. Thankfully, miraculously, an old Marshallese man and his younger cousin revived the art.

The old man, you see, had been trained as a *ri-meto*, or "person of the sea," as a boy but didn't actually get his official title from the island's chief as was the tradition because he had not taken the test because of the hydrogen bomb testing. For thousands of years, *ri-metos* were minted on the islands. They would learn the art then get pushed out to sea and have to find their way to some island or another on their first try. If they didn't make it, they would die alone under the stars, sharks circling. If they shared their secrets to any non *ri-meto,* they would be killed on land. In any case, the art was reading the refracted swell that bounced off the islands and atolls. To be able to read these patterns of swirl in the middle of the ocean through sight, but mostly by feel. They would lie on their backs, eyes closed, feeling the chop hit the canoe and know how far land was and which direction it was and where to go.

No wonder the first Europeans supposed the hand of God dropped people and the godless scientists believed in sunken continents—because both make more sense than reading wave chop by feel way out at sea.

The old man, anyhow, knew the art would die with him if he didn't do anything, so he got a special dispensation from his chief to be able to teach his younger cousin...and I'm sorry to be so far down a baroque segue here, but have you ever been out on the Pacific? Like deep Pacific, away from any land? It's a giant desert. A blue pancake of blinding light and the occasional breeching whale. It is impossible for the human mind to comprehend, and yet the ancient Polynesians and Micronesians danced upon it like they were following waltz steps marked out on a floor.

And so the old man's knowledge got passed on to his younger cousin, and three scientists watched the man navigate by feeling the wave refractions and wept, if I recall, as they witnessed a miracle. A total marvel, and just one of many marvelous tales of Micronesian and Polynesian navigation.

Or maybe it is a marvel only to me, and mostly because my directional sense is absolutely terrible. Even on land. Even in a place I have lived for years. Especially in places I have never been. I am a liability. A blight. I was once in Kiev, for example, directly after those fiery Iron *Maidan* protests of 2013. My "bridge-burning" surf book had just come out and I thought I was back on my way to a meaningful destiny. I did not yet know I was running from it.

My phone was not working because and thus I was Google Maps-less—but wanting to get into the mix, I pushed off into the charred drizzle with nothing but *joie de vivre* and a fantastic pair of Saint Laurent sunglasses. Before long I was hopelessly lost and stuck in some weird barracks of a protester practicing swordplay, mumbling what he was going to do to the Russians when they returned, swishing his blade right under my nose. I didn't know where I was and I tried to leave, but he wouldn't let me unless I knew where I was going—because the Russians. And was I on their side? Was I on their team? Why was I wearing sunglasses? I asked for tea, eventually, and when he went to make it in a broken-down Volga he was using as a kitchen, I ran out into the streets but got more lost and had to spend time with two Ukrainians dressed as Eastern European Mickey Mouses who proceeded to bore me with broken English and folk dances.

Scientists call it the "neurological effect of navigation by smartphone." Scientists say that our directional sense lives where our memory does, and when we wend around by using technology instead of our brains, we quite basically give ourselves Alzheimer's. That we never really know where we are in the world and that puts humanity's very future in danger. All I know is that I am an absolute directional catastrophe and that my memory really is so bad that I've been accused of Alzheimer's more than once and I blame navigating by my phone. Or playing football in seventh and eighth grade as the skinniest boy ever born.

It is a nasty son of a bitch and I sometimes wish I were an ancient Polynesian because they could sail but also because they had gorgeous tattoos and it makes perfect sense, in the end, that a people who were able to understand the ocean so intimately, who navigated by the feeling of her undulations, would find pleasure in her waves. Would understand them enough to ride them. To have fun on them. To bring surfing to each and every island they discovered.

The crew of Captain James Cook are likely the first Europeans to ever witness surfing when the *HMS Endeavour* sailed past Tahiti during the summer of 1769, though Dr. Ben Finney, a Harvard-educated Pacific historian, suggests that proto-Polynesians had been surfing for a thousand or so years. It was a kids' game except on Marquesas, Tahiti, Hawaii, the Cook Islands, and New Zealand, where adults also rode waves. Only Tahitians and Hawaiians rode while standing, though, and only Hawaiians turned it into a national obsession starting around 1500 AD.

It is a romantic tale that adds color to the scale-eyed surfer. Maybe even a little bit of depth. Surfing was an activity of great kings. Of conquerors. It traveled across the mighty Pacific from point to point as if by magic on the wings of men and women who felt the ocean with their bodies, with their souls. It is a beautiful ancient dance, and the surfer a beautiful ancient dancer.

And now somehow I've accidentally wandered back over to Fifth Street. I can hear the empty din emanating from the Shorebreak's deck, floating down the street, and can't remember where I parked my car.

Ugh. I need to leave. I need to drive and forget this cursed life, so I fish my iPhone out of my pocket, but it flips out of my APC raw jeans that I only just washed for the first time in two years yesterday so they are twice as skinny and the phone smashes into the ground.

Shit.

I look toward the heavens, toward the Author of my Fate, before bending over to grab my for-sure cracked iPhone and realize I'm standing in front of Huntington Beach's International Surfing Museum. What are the fucking odds? I mean, that an "International Surfing Museum" exists is weird, sure, but that the dark night of my soul takes me right to it? In the window there is a black-and-white picture of some South American mestizo-looking thing, grinning broadly, riding what appears to be a strange surfboard. Written in bold font it says, "Surfing and Peru. 4,000 years."

I freeze and feel the blood draining from my face. Did surfing actually start in Peru? Didn't cocaine?

Shit.

3

Supernatural Aid!

I couldn't turn my mind off that night. I'd somehow found my car using the decidedly not-ancient Polynesian method of pressing my key's panic button until I heard the alarm wail, then driven home from Huntington Beach and the International Surfing Museum and the strange Peruvian as fast as my Volkswagen would carry me. Past Newport, Laguna, San Clemente, Camp Pendleton, Oceanside, Carlsbad, to Cardiff by the Sea. In a mental fog, spinning.

My wife was, thankfully, asleep when I got home. She would have been worried about me. I was worried about me. What the hell? Have surfing and cocaine really been locked in loving embrace since the beginning of recorded time? Really? And if yes, how has this story never been written?

Am I God's vessel? There's no way I'm God's vessel because there is no way surfing *actually* started in Peru. Right? And there is no way God likes cocaine. Right? Isn't there a Bible verse about not being shallow? There totally is. The parable of the sower where some of his seeds fall in good soil, some fall in no soil, and some fall in shallow soil. Isn't the shallow soil worst of all? I think it must be—but, Peru. I don't know if surfing *really* started there but I know someone who does, though he lives in Seattle, Washington, of all places and is also an atheist. He dwells in a place where the sun literally doesn't shine. A place with no surf but dramatic suicides. A place with very minimal God and probably deep soil.

The next day I make the worst pot of French press coffee, which shoots all over the zinc kitchen counter that I had insisted upon, aesthetically, even though sea air attaches to zinc and corrodes it almost instantly. I drop my iPhone, again, sending an already broken piece flying off into my young daughter's toys. I forget to pick my wife's daughter up from soccer practice because I am trying to research surf history online. And I know, by evening, there is only one way out.

I have to go to Seattle. I have to see Matt Warshaw. He will fix me. He will set me straight.

I tell my wife I need twenty-four hours, that I am in the middle of an existential crisis and need answers. She can see the madness in my eyes and grants me leave. I book an Alaska Airlines flight, snag a rental car, drive through the rain and into an air of annoyance as the waiter in this wood-paneled, iron-railing'd, reclaimed Queen Anne restaurant I have arrived at is impatiently tapping his pen on his notebook waiting for me to decide between a whiskey soda and a Moscow Mule. He suggested a Kentucky Mule five minutes ago thinking it was an easy solution to my dilemma. "Hey, mix it together and get a Kentucky Mule. Problem solved." Except my problem is not solved because I don't want a Kentucky Mule. I either want a whiskey drink or a vodka drink. Not a whiskey drink masquerading as a vodka drink.

Matt Warshaw sits across from me drinking a glass of Sauvignon blanc and smirking. His smirk is an almost permanent fixture these days and I suppose it would be for me too if I were a surf historian instead of a surf journalist.

Surf historian. Surf. Historian.

Surf.   Historian.

The ludicrousness makes "surf journalist" sound positively sensible. But he is why I had to come all the way to Seattle. He is the way I drop this romantic nonsense and go back to simple self-loathing.

Overall he almost looks the historian part. Natty with a sensible gray T-shirt under a slightly darker gray sweater from maybe Brooks Bros. Black specs with a serious, heavy frame. A stylistic nod to Kevin

Costner as he appeared in JFK, perhaps, but not on the nose at all. Subtle. Scholarly. Well kept.

Except inside there is something clearly wrong with him in the same way there is something clearly wrong with me in the way there is something clearly wrong with all surfers. A madness in his eyes— alongside the markings of pterygium.

He keeps smirking as the waiter keeps impatiently tapping his pen as I keep saying, "Uhhhhhhhhhhh..." and as I look from the menu to the waiter to him, I feel his smirk is even more pronounced than the last time we spent time together. A little different. A little more aggressive. What is it? What's different? And then it dawns on me. *The New Yorker* had just made him their Talk of the Town. *The New Yorker.* As in the crème of polite society's crop. Esteemed by the upwardly mobile liberal and downwardly unmovable conservative alike.

A surf historian. The Talk of the Town.

He was described thusly:

Warshaw is the world's leading surfing scholar, the Linnaeus of the lineup. Over the years, he has assembled a research library, in his home, of hundreds of books, thousands of periodicals, and some 350 movies, and created a database: logged, indexed, searchable.

And can you believe that? Can you even believe it? Amazing. The honor that kicked him over the line, I think, was being named the Oxford English Dictionary's official surf vocabulary consultant. Can you believe that too? I almost can't.

When I first read that sentence in *The New Yorker,* I read it the "Linus of the lineup" as opposed to the "Linnaeus of the lineup." As in Charlie Brown's pal who always carried the blanket. As in Lucy's younger brother. And I wondered what in the world Linus had to do with surf or with Matt Warshaw. Later I looked up Linnaeus and discovered he was the Swede who came up with binomial nomenclature, the two-part Latin system the world uses to categorize every living species. Like *Homo sapiens, Felis catus,* etc.

Matt Warshaw was supposed to be too good for this. Bred to be too good for this. His lineage was built out of famous scholars and proper, culturally verifiable intelligence. Grandfather a PhD from the Sorbonne, mother a PhD from UCLA, father a mathematics genius and physicist at Rand Corp. with brothers and uncles—and maybe another grandfather—successful personalities at the University of Chicago and Columbia. Most of the family found their way to California though, as intelligent people do, and set up shop.

"My family had all this cool LA shit," he tells me after I decide on a Kon-Tiki, sending the waiter away with a look of bewildered semi-annoyance. "All this smart, liberal, cool LA shit that they were doing, all of which I was completely ignorant of because when I started surfing at age eight I didn't give a shit. None of it meant anything to me. I didn't care about any of it. It's all this stuff that I find out way, way, way later, how cool my family is…but at the time I was just out blithely surfing and not paying attention. I was probably, looking back, expected to go to a good university, but I went to San Diego State and you go to fucking San Diego State to surf and drink beer and that's what I did for a year and then I quit. That was too fucking rigorous for me, right? And I started working at a surf shop and that's when my mom kicked me out of the house."

Matt's genetic intelligence couldn't stay buried forever and the strands of smart DNA had begun to twist around his surf addiction. He worked at that surf shop and parlayed that into a job writing for *Surfer* magazine then became its editor-in-chief and was getting paid well and living the good life, but his intelligence began to revolt against the emptiness, the shallowness, the pointlessness, the "where-do-I-put-my-hands-in-the-water?" so he quit and enrolled at UC Berkley and proceeded to get his history degree before going to UCLA to get his PhD in history. And then the revolt of his intelligence was beat back by the powerful forces that lurk in the shallow end, so he dropped out again to chase the surf life to become, as *The New Yorker* put it better than I ever could have, the "Linnaeus of the lineup." A surf historian. The world's first and only surf historian. He has written the—two-hundred-thousand—word *Encyclopedia of Surfing* and the equally lengthy *History of Surfing*. He has a scholar's mind and a surfer's hollowness. And I need to ask him an important question right now. A question so important that it necessitated a trip up to Seattle. A question that my future hinges upon.

The waiter sets down my Kon-Tiki with needless aggression, still upset, I think, that I didn't take his very sensible suggestion and veered so off course into the realm of rum plus scotch plus Cointreau. I take a sip and marvel how good they mingle, look at Matt, and say, "Surfing didn't really begin in Hawaii, did it?"

Matt scrunches his nose slightly while adjusting his appropriately toned-down Kevin Costner JFK specs.

"It didn't begin in Tahiti either," I continue. "It didn't begin anywhere in the gorgeous tropical Pacific, with its sheer beauty being such that it could, in theory and over time, render vision superfluous. Did it..." and I'm not asking "Did it?" I'm saying "did it" because I want Matt to laugh at me. I want him to prove me wrong, to look at me like I am a total idiot. I want that more than anything but I know in the deepest part of my heart, and by the look on his face, that I am right. That I am fucking right.

The Norwegian Thor Heyerdahl, you see, came up with a seemingly wild hypothesis in the early 1940s. He believed that it was a pre-Incan race from Peru that first populated Polynesia. That they had somehow sailed thousands of miles across the Pacific and set up camp. That Polynesians were Peruvians a few thousand years removed. The scholarship of the time was conclusive. Polynesia was first settled from China downward and westward and it was absurd to believe anything else.

But Thor was a romantic and had heard an Incan legend that suggested that a white-skinned people once lived in Peru and were ruled by the sun god named Kon-Tiki. They built magnificent stone structures and were very modern but, as happens, were attacked by a group of bearded white-skinned people and brutally massacred. (Ask anyone who lives in Brooklyn or Venice Beach about this regularly occurring phenomenon.) Kon-Tiki managed to escape with some of his closest friends. They made it to the shore—which was ugly, cold, perpetually shrouded in cold mist—then pushed out to sea and were never seen again.

When the Spaniards first came to Peru, Heyerdahl unearthed notes suggesting the ruling Incans told their new guests that the magnificent deserted ruins were built before their time by white gods who had fled westward across the Pacific never to return.

The first European explorers to set foot on certain of the Pacific Islands did, in fact, find that the natives there were shockingly white, some even having blonde hair. And while it all sounds very Mormon-ish, Heyerdahl believed that it was some Neolithic Peruvian people who were the first ever from Hawaii to New Zealand and all of Polynesia in between.

He gathered linguistic, archeological, and anthropological evidence that supported his claim. Polynesia has sweet potatoes, for example. Sweet potatoes that genetically come from Peru. Some DNA evidence gathered in 2011 even suggests a Polynesian-Peruvian link.

Still, most scientists scoffed in large part because how in the world could the ancient Peruvians have sailed across the Pacific, all the way across the entire thing, in their primitive little rafts?

Thor dug up any bit of information he could on Incan rafts by reading early Spanish accounts and studying archeological evidence. In 1947, he and five brave Norwegian souls pushed off from Peru's shores on a balsa wood raft they had named Kon-Tiki. Some 101 days and 4,300 nautical miles later, they smashed into the Tuamotu Islands. Polynesia. Islands, coincidentally, with amazing surf.

They filmed the entire adventure and won 1951's Academy Award for Best Feature Documentary. More importantly, though, he proved that it was very possible for a trip of that magnitude to be made.

But what was life like in ancient Peru? If it is true, if they were the first to settle Polynesia, what did they bring with them besides whiter skin and sweet potatoes? What were they doing besides building magnificent stone structures on that ugly shore?

Oh, but they were surfing, of course.

Surfing without palm trees, without blue water, without rainbows without beauty and probably in knit hats. Surfing since the very beginning of recorded time. Maybe since even 3000 BC. Getting their stoke on thousands of years before any footprints, Mormon or other, scarred Polynesia's rose-colored sand. Surfing just like they were in the International Surfing Museum's window.

Archeological interest in South America took a bit longer to establish than, say, Egypt or Greece, but when scientists started scratching the dirt, they discovered magnificent wonders like Machu Picchu, which was coincidentally stumbled upon by a Hawaiian with a Mormon-ish name: Hiram Bingham III. And El Paraíso, which had been a booming coastal metropolis in 4000 BC and Guietarrero Cave, which had been a Peruvian party spot since 10,000 BC, and Caral with magnificent pyramids older than the ones in Egypt.

They discovered drawings of little horses too or *caballitos*. The caballito was not a flesh-and-blood actual little horse but rather a boat made up of a bundle of reeds maybe six feet long, squared at one end and flipped up on its other. Like an extra-chubby surfboard. Peru's fishermen have been using the *caballito* since at least 3,000 BC to fish, move goods between coastal villages, and surf. And to surf at least a thousand years before the Polynesians.

To be fair, their surfing consisted mostly of cruising the shore break to the beach after a day's fishing or moving goods, but there are ancient ceramic sculptures of Peruvians perched on caballitos, heads down with broad, empty smiles stretching from ear to ear, clearly surfing.

And did these pre-Peruvian fisherman bring surfing with them when they set off across the mighty Pacific thousands of years ago? Is this the heart of surfing? And if an ugly, cold coast is the heart of surfing, then where did eye scales come from?

Matt is not laughing at me. He is trying to control his smirk as he rolls up one sleeve of his sensible sweater, takes a sip of his Sauvignon blanc, and says, "No, no. it's just…it's just fishermen coming in from a day's catch and laying their paddles down to ride a wave in and thinking, 'Oh that feels kind of good.' It's like if you had to ride your bike home from work every day and the last two hundred yards of your ride is downhill to your driveway. That's awesome. 'I'm done with my job now, just let me put me feet up on my handlebars and ride down the hill.' I guess surfing needs to be something more, or at least it does to me, by definition. It needs to be its own thing. You're designing a craft *for* surfing. And you're going out into the water *to* surf. That's where I would draw the distinction. If you're talking about where we come from, obsessing about surfing and standing up on waves on boards... my gut tells me there is no other way that it makes sense except for it having come from Hawaii."

But I see that his heart is not in his explanation as I take another sip of my Kon-Tiki. And this is why I had to come to Seattle instead of just calling him up on the phone. I had to see his reaction with my own eyes, and now that I have, I know that Matt Warshaw, the Linnaeus of the lineup, a surf historian—surfing's *only* historian—is wrong. I can feel that he is wrong.

His eyes are betraying him. Damned pterygium.

He is the first to admit that surf history is an oral game told and retold and eventually turned into myth. He even once wrote, "Demythologizing the sport, in fact, was another great goal of mine. I couldn't wait to sledge away at the cheerleading and boosterism and perjured nobility layered onto most of the surf history. Pulling down shoddy historiographic handicraft is, by itself, I admit, pretty satisfying. But the real purpose—and the real pleasure—comes from the fact that the mortal, ground-level version of events is, almost without exception, more compelling than the legend or the myth."

Now I smirk for the first time since seeing that damned Peruvian poster. I take another sip and chuckle inside, except even more bitterly. Look at the surf historian listening to his gut over the facts. God bless him for still being a surfer above all else. A surfer so addicted that he had to move to Seattle, Washington, in order to remove the temptation and raise a son, but he is wrong.

Part of me, though, wishes I could listen to my gut, too. That I could kick Thor Heyerdahl and his merry men from my heart forever, because a menace lies in his story. Kon-Tiki was remade as a feature film in 2012 starring Gustaf Skarsgård, who plays Floki on the History Channel's brilliant *Vikings*. He's the crazy one with the amazing eye

46

shadow, but not the dreamiest of dreamies, which is Ragnar Lodbrok, played by the Australia's Travis Fimmel, with his braided hair and his perfect nose and his bluest eyes. A man so handsome that I sometimes fear my wife will leave me for him.

I wish I could listen to my gut, like Matt, and flush horrible new plans away, but I can't because I already know. Riding a wave is surfing. It is a simple, scientific definition. The most pure essence. Intention has nothing to do with it and yes, Polynesia is gorgeous. It is so gorgeous that any stumbling shallowness grown there can be forgiven. Peru's coast, again, is not beautiful. It is not beautiful by any definition either scientific or romantic. Ugly. Cold. Perpetually shrouded in cold mist. And so if it was not beauty that stole the surfer's eye, then what was it?

I will tell you. It was cocaine. And the world's most endearingly degenerate love story just turned into its oldest. And I am the one destined to write it and if I write it right it will make surfing great again because surfers everywhere will have to admit exactly what they are. That they are not soulful dancers or athletes or sportsmen or watermen. They are addicts. We are addicts. And if we can all admit that we are addicts, then surfing can shrug off the thing that is holding it down. It can shrug off the staid conservatism from the Disney and NFL executive vision and free itself from the apocalypse.

I can't sit here listening to this Seattle atheist any longer. I can't run like Jonah in the Bible. It is time to accept my fate.

I am a surf journalist.

4

Road of Trials and Tests!

I fly back to San Diego, smashed in a middle seat between a chunky Denver Broncos superfan reading *unPHILtered*, the collected thoughts of that old *Duck Dynasty* patriarch, and a lesbian. Or I think she's a lesbian because she is listening to Indigo Girls so loudly that I can hear it and pairing Doc Martens with denim shorts.

The drink cart clinks down the aisle, waddled by a kind steward with an almost perfect moustache. I order two mini Tito's bottles and one can of soda and end up knocking into both *Duck Dynasty* and Indigo Girl while trying to pry my wallet from my still-too-tight jeans. Both glare slightly and edge away, leaving me an armrest on each side.

Since I forgot to bring a book and didn't have time to buy a magazine, I am left to drink and ponder this sudden turn in my life, the journey I am about to embark upon. And why has surfing and cocaine's ancient love story stayed relatively hidden for so many years? Why is now the time for it to be revealed to the world? Is it because we live in such painfully divisive times, with the left fighting the right and the poor fighting the rich and the healthy eating the sick? Could this love story, beyond freeing the surf industry from its nasty conservative shackles, bring us all together the way that Romeo and Juliet brought together the Montagues and Capulets? I look over at *Duck Dynasty*, who has fallen asleep, then at Indigo Girl, who is ripping into her Northwest

Deli Picnic Pack. Can cocaine and surfing's bond against impossible odds unite even these two?

The plane lands before I can engage either in conversation and test the love story's cathartic properties in our polarized era though, in truth, I was probably overreaching. Surfing, and what happens in surfing, only matters to surfers.

I switch my phone off airplane mode and its broken screen fills with messages.

"You coming?"

"Hey bro...come!"

"Wanna drive together?"

"COME!"

I'm confused until I check my emails and see that tonight is the death party for *Surfing*. Yesterday, after fifty-three years, the magazine had officially closed its doors, a victim of the general surf industry apocalypse. The Reign of Terror. Print is dying everywhere and particularly in the surf industry, where the apocalypse guts budgets, but neither of those things actually killed *Surfing*.

Surfer killed it.

The two are, or were, owned by the same group and the gutless babies at *Surfer* always felt threatened, so they went crying to the publisher and wept, "Us or them!" Since the publisher had just diversified its portfolio by turning *Surfer* into a chain of bars, it was a seemingly easy decision.

I was a "retained writer" at *Surfing* for a few years back when "retainers" still existed, then the "editor-at-living-large" for a few more years—a mostly pretend title that suited my mostly pretend contributions. I always brought the absolute worst ideas to the table. Like dedicating an entire issue to the graphic designer's son because his name was Pablo and he had an amazing blonde afro. Or rerunning issues from ten years ago word for word and seeing if anyone noticed. My high watermark, probably, was going to Florida and sneaking into the 2012 Republican National Convention by promising some drunk southern party boss the surf vote, then writing a story about Mitt Romney's mouth.

And I am about to respond, "Hell no!" to the party invites. I am not sentimental and don't feel in the mood for empty surf chats and would rather watch an episode of *Vikings*, damn that hunky Ragnar Lodbrok, but stop myself because I remember that I have a new journey, a new calling, and so I drive from San Diego to San Clemente. I call my wife as I pass Cardiff by the Sea and explain that I have to go to a quick surf party. She sounds too understanding.

She is probably going to watch that damn hunky Ragnar Lodbrok all by herself.

But I can't let jealousies get in the way of my new journey and I pull into the parking lot of Molly Bloom's Irish Bar thirty minutes later. A surf journalist. I don't know what, exactly, I'm looking for here, but I assume whatever it is will find me.

Pushing through the door, I am once again enveloped in a scene that has played out the exact same for the past forever. A messy knot of people pushing toward the bar and toward the bathroom with equal force. Too close, too loud for talking. Too much talking. Nose rubbing. Chatty, conspiratorial, ecstatic, depressed, ecstatic, chatty. Conspiratorial.

It's always snowing in Orange County, or so they say.

I try to press toward the bar but am intercepted by a very dapper industry bro holding an extra vodka-something. I take it from him and he says, "Yeah, Chas…" while nodding slowly and flashing a half smile. In another world his face would belong to a heartthrob singer or an actor or a model, or at the very least a teeth model. His teeth are impossibly straight and white. I would have assumed that they are veneers but they are not. They are real and blindingly white and so straight. I can't take my eyes off of them and probably look weird when I respond, "Howzit…" while staring at his mouth.

In another world his very handsome face would be pinned to the bedroom walls of teenaged girls or orthodontists. In this world, it does sales for the surf forecasting website *Surfline* and before that it was surf team manager for a surf shoe brand called Globe.

And surf industry genetics are a thing to behold. Inside it may seem the surf industry bro is a vacuum, an empty vessel, even though his heart is racing for his true and ancient love. Outside, though, he is almost perfect. Always lean, always tan, always well proportioned, always salty ideally tousled hair, though usually a little short.

Why? The surf industry bro doesn't grow food or build things or know things. Why, then, has evolution gifted such a worthless cultural appendage such genetic superiority? I don't really know, though think it has something to do with the surf industry's Mecca being Orange County. A place that molds its population after itself: pretty and vapid.

This particular surf industry bro, the one with the beyond handsome face and perfect teeth, and I chat empty surf talk for a minute. "You surf today? Sick. Where?" etc., and then he asks me what I'm working on next—after "that Hawaii book."

I tell him, "Cocaine plus surfing…it's a love story."

His nod doesn't change rhythm nor does his smile change intensity and he says, "Yeah. Well, you won't have any shortage of material," before pushing off into the sweaty pit.

I watch, thinking about his teeth and wondering what career avenues open for a man with perfect teeth, but those thoughts are interrupted by an angry mouth too close to my ear. "These fuckers. These fucking fuckers taking *Surfing* away from us…fucking…fuckers. They wanted us to fail so they could shift our image archive away and sell it for millions of dollars and fuck us out of our rights. Now they won't have to pay us, any of us, for reusing shots. Fucking…"

A damned surf photographer. I nod and say, "Yeah, totally," before shuffling back toward the bar. I want to leave already but am really trying to honor my journey, trying to be a good surf journalist for the first time in my life. Trying to uncover little specifics in the world's greatest love story. Like, asking people questions and stuff. I just got done asking *Surfing*'s ex--Editor in Chief, Taylor Paul, if he likes cocaine. He looked at me all pucker-faced and said, "No. Are you kidding me? I hate the stuff. It makes everyone so…lame."

I suppose he is the exception to the rule.

After all, he is from Santa Cruz, and most Santa Cruz surfers love methamphetamine.

I'd just got done asking an intern who works for the extreme sport sock company Stance if she has any cocaine. She said no while looking at me like I was a total idiot by subverting the social order. I was supposed to be telling her I had cocaine. Stance is one of the only companies thriving in the surf space, though, so I thought it was a fair question.

I then ask a part-time professional surfer, part-time DJ if he wants cocaine. He says, "Sure..." then gets angry when I tell him I don't have any.

And I *really* should have left an hour ago. It is too late and now I am depressed and caught in the conspiratorial web of another surf photographer who is even more furious than the last that *Surfing Magazine* got shut down and is insisting that the magazine was actually making money and doing well. The crowd is still thick and getting sloppy.

It would be impossible to guess if his rant, or the rant before his, is cocaine-infused because most surf photographers are, by nature, conspiratorial. Someone is always stealing their art. No one is ever paying them enough. Everyone in this whole damned industry has profited and profited handsomely except them. In their collective mind, they are getting fucked. Always getting fucked and always ready to snap about it, though I once carried a surf photographer's backpack across a mile of beach and instantly understood surf photographer rage. The backpack weighed 250 pounds. The sand was scorching hot. It was like a forced march and all surf photographers should be paid reparations by the brands for their servitude.

"...fucking saw one of my shots being used by fucking Rip Curl on their Instagram feed...gonna fucking kill someone..."

The surf photographer rage and victimization complex is extreme but also mirrors the way most surfers feel about the surf industry. Surfers love surfing and reckon it such a pure love. Such a rush, such a kick. Such a high. But then they start looking around and seeing more and more people riding waves alongside them and they turn into strange possessive Gollums, hating other surfers, stealing their waves, getting high off their waves, fucking other surfers and hating the industry that is built around selling their personal dream. So much like the last boy with a baggie of cocaine at a dying party. Such hiding in the bathroom. Such suspicion of everyone and everything.

I run into a rep—or "brand representative"—who is old now and has slowly slid down the pole of relevant brands, from Rip Curl wetsuits to On A Mission surfboard bags and is now shilling wax and skateboards. He should know better. He should have gotten out forever ago but this whole damned surf thing is a trap and he asks me, "You seen Dill-dog? Somebody said that bro is here but I swear he Christian Baled an hour ago. How's that? I told him this party was gonna be on like *Donkey Kong*…"

He starts to trail off but is also an autodidact so I ask him, "What is the history of cocaine?"

He rubs his nose and says, "Started in three-K BC, broski."

I say "cool" then quickly Google "cocaine," while he starts to behave inappropriately in front of a waitress, and see that he is right.

Coca has been a part of South America since at least 3000 BC, pretty much the same day as surfing. The tree, short and stubby with fiery-red berries and electric-green leaves, grew natively at the base of the majestic Andes in what we now call Ecuador, Peru, Bolivia, and Colombia, and has been a continuous part of coastal ancient life throughout the northern part of the continent for literally ever. Depictions or actual carbon traces of coca are found in art, mummies, sculpture, ceramic pots, and little satchels.

There is no definitive scientific theory about how it got there, but Amerigo Vespucci, the Italian explorer for whom the whole land is named—both North and South—spotted it straight away on his first visit in 1499 and wrote:

We descried an island that lay about 15 leagues from the coast and decided to go there to see if it was inhabited. We found there the most bestial and ugly people we had ever seen: very ugly of face and expression, and all of them had their cheeks full of a green herb that they chewed constantly like beasts, so they could barely speak. Each one carried around his neck two gourds, one of them full of that herb and the other of a white powder that looked like pulverized plaster. They dipped a stick into the powder, and then put the stick in the mouth, in order to apply powder to the herb that they chewed; they did this frequently. We were amazed at this and could not understand its secret or why they did it.

And since at least 3000 BC, these pre-Incans, these Valdivians, had been toying with their dopamine levels. They had been using the coca leaf for all manner of reasons, both mundane and sacred. It is even suggested that it was the very first plant to be cultivated in the Americas. These earliest men would use the leaf to stave off hunger, to keep altitude sickness at bay, to give energy, and to cure disease. Priests would use coca, ritually, to protect from curses, change bad luck, predict the future, and make offerings to Mother Earth—whom they called Pachamama.

The Spanish, when they first began establishing colonies in this new world, for example, brought their Catholicism with them and the Catholic priests did not like this coca-chewing ritual offering to Mother Earth or any of its attachment to the pagan gods. They thought it would be better if the plant were eradicated altogether but understood its value in keeping the native population working.

Local traditions had it that buying and selling coca was blasphemy, frowned upon by the gods, but the Spanish overrode that with the Church's blessing. They did not care what lowercase "g" gods wanted, and so they seeded the world's first large-scale coca plantations, paid the natives in coca, and became the New World's first proper drug dealers.

A Spanish contemporary is noted saying in Colombian professor Jorge Bejarano's *New Chapters on Cocainism*, "Our fair-minded masters do not want the poor to recognize their tragedy, and wish instead that they should die without realizing their hunger and their ignorance; that the bitter taste of coca might dull the instinct to rebel, and that they might live in an artificial paradise."

The chewers, thus, didn't need as much food and were kept warm and altitude sickness-free and docile and happy even a million feet underground and very close to hell. They were mining silver and gold, digging deep into that Mother Earth, sending the riches across the seas to masters they had never met nor heard of. They worked torturous hours with wives and children starving outside but with relaxed faces and relaxed spirits.

Relaxed faces and relaxed spirits.

Surfing and cocaine have truly come to look like each other in the same way that a longtime dog owner will begin to resemble his mutt, and maybe because there they were together in Peru. Mingling for three thousand, four thousand years before anyone even peeked in on them. Dancing some early, partially forgotten dance. Belonging to each other from the very beginning.

There is an ancient creation story about coca that the tree was once the most beautiful woman on Earth, so gorgeous that all the wave-riding fishermen fought over her. Since not everyone could have her, the elders turned her into a plant so she could be enjoyed by everyone equally. But then, like in any great love epic, the two were split. Torn apart by forces out of their control. Surfing went to Polynesia. It was embraced by the Tahitians then really embraced by the Hawaiians. It was changed and reordered and reset and remade. And coca went to Europe.

Those early Spanish settlers busily exported new and fascinating plants they discovered back home. Coffee and its future Starbucks, tobacco and its Marlboro Red, chocolate and its Hershey's. The Old World fell in love with these fabulous products and the magic properties they contained, but somehow the most magical of these stayed behind.

It has been hypothesized that coca chewers looked like cows munching cud and the aesthetic turnoff was great enough for conquistadors to find no real interest in it outside of suppressing the native masses. Whatever the reason, the coca bush was left alone until 1855. But then the world cracked.

Scientists had begun to isolate compounds in plants, pulling them out and allowing them to pop in full. Morphine in 1804, caffeine in 1819, codeine in 1832, cocaine in 1855. The German chemist Friedrich Gaedcke isolated the specific cocaine alkaloid and published his findings in a journal read by another German chemist, Friedrich Wöhler, who in turn asked a colleague on an Austrian boat traveling around the world to bring him loads of coca leaves. The colleague agreed, and Wöhler passed the leaves on to his German chemist friend, Albert Niemann, who then fixed the purification process and wrote his University of Göttingen dissertation titled Über eine neue organische Base in den Cocablättern or *On a New Organic Base in the Coca Leaves,* which he published in 1860.

Dr. Niemann's first description of this newly isolated and purified alkaloid was less than poetic. He simply wrote, "Its solutions have an alkaline reaction, a bitter taste, promote the flow of saliva and leave a peculiar numbness, followed by a sense of cold when applied to the tongue." He named his alkaloid cocaine, borrowing "coca–" from South America and "–ine" from the stylistic way of describing local anesthetics of the day.

Coca–

–ine.

Cocaine.

And it all seems very cleanly scientific, no? Very "modern man extrapolating into the future," except the isolation of cocaine from the coca plant did something far greater.

Tom Feiling, a Colombian hip-hop documentarian and cocaine scholar, wrote, "This isolation was not only a chemical process: it also sheared psychoactive substances from their specific cultural context. They could now be packaged as commodities, and sold to anyone with the money to buy them. Since these substances were no longer dispensed by healers, or reserved for special ceremonies, people had to learn how to take drugs all over again."

And there went cocaine from Peru to Europe, getting isolated and purified and freed from its cow-like cultural context. And there went surfing from Peru to Polynesia, standing up and getting nude and becoming a full, wild obsession.

Like *The Princess Bride.* Remember? The very pretty farm girl, Buttercup (played by the gorgeous Robin Wright pre-Penn), and the handsome stable boy, Westley (played by the dashing Cary Elwes), fell in love as poverty-stricken youth. Semi-weird/not sexy in the farm/barn context. Cow shit and fetching water from the well and feeding goats and collecting eggs and discordant power situation, etc. Circumstances took them away from each other, though, and while they seemed rough at the time, Buttercup was made a radiant princess and Westley a pirate wearing the best black blindfold that has maybe ever been worn, or at least the best one that has been worn by someone other than John Galliano. They both turned gorgeous.

And what if Buttercup and Westley had never been separated? I'll tell you what. They would have gotten married and had kids, voted for populist candidates, eaten hot dogs, and lived on the farm surrounded by cow shit and goats and chickens. Their children would have fetched water from the well and eggs from the chickens and would have fed those goats, but no. That is not a real love story. A real love story transcends. Buttercup and Westley both transcended and were able to overcome the Fire Swamp, Prince Humperdinck, André the Giant, a priest with a speech impediment, and death in order to swing from the most glorious heights.

Surfing and cocaine needed to be separated from each other to find their best selves, or at least their truest selves. But nothing can keep true loves away, and the very alluring, albeit dull, cocaine and the very obsessed surfing were sure to reconnect.

The social media manager for a different surf magazine that is trying to follow *Surfing* into the grave bumbles past all sweaty and hot. I ask him if he loves cocaine. He turns toward me, his face becoming a menacing scowl, and he says, "You'd better not write anything about me, Chas. You'd better not, you fucking dick. Everyone hates you..." before storming off.

I guess he does.

5

Belly of the Whale!

I drive home from *Surfing Magazine*'s wake maybe drunk, but isn't that the way you are supposed to come home from a wake at an Irish bar and an open-casket funeral? I've watched *Snatch* enough to know. Wait. Was Brad Pitt Irish in *Snatch*? He was, wasn't he? I can't remember. Irish or maybe Welsh?

The next few weeks, in any case, morph back into my standard, pre-divine appointment, surf-journalist grind. I pen instant classics such as, "Surfers who should have died at 27!" and "Hot: World's first trans trans surfer!" while trying to grasp a receding narrative of surfing and her cocaine. The world's first trans trans surfer story was actually interesting. An Australian surf champ from the 1970s named Peter Drouyn decided to transition to Westerly Wendina a few years ago. He changed clothes, fingernail polish, dress, hair, and became very beautiful. A blonde bombshell. Then it was time for the final change but, after hemming and hawing for a while, decided that she wanted to be Peter Drouyn again and came out, as his old self, at a Gold Coast surf awards show. The great Jamie Brisick wrote a book about this adventure titled *Finding Westerly*.

And like Peter Drouyn almost lost his thread, I'm almost losing mine. What happened to cocaine and surfing after they got separated? Where did they go? I can't really concentrate because, right now, a loud man from Ohio is smashing into me at Duke's Barefoot Bar in Huntington Beach telling his wife that there was a shark sighting near the pier last week but that he learned on *Shark Week* that great white shark attacks on humans are actually down this year overall but "hell with it, anyway. Gonna rent a board tomorrow and give it a whirl."

I came to Huntington to meet with a surf filmmaker that I was supposed to do a story on but he blew me off and I was sitting on the pier with no date and decided to be an asshole and go to Duke's. I don't actually know if the man sitting next to me is from Ohio, either, but he is wearing a bright red Ohio Buckeyes cap and also a brand-new Billabong T-shirt, which is he pronouncing *Billabonic*. "I wonder if they got Billabonic boards down there at the beach rental place?" His wife gives a passive shrug and takes a sip of her mai tai. She's wearing a brand-new T-shirt that reads, "Huntington Beach, CA. Surf City, USA!"

I take a sip of my mai tai also and smile. This sort of surf mockery, this utter kookiness, used to annoy me badly because in my deepest heart I knew it was not too far off from my own cold Oregonian root. I used to guffaw, point and laugh, mock. I used to make fun of the man who strapped a surfboard to the car fins down in an effort to cook the barney from my own soul, but at some point I realized it is there forever no matter how much fun I make of others. I'm a surf journalist sitting at the Barefoot Bar in Duke's Huntington Beach next to corn-fed yokels drinking instead of interviewing a surf filmmaker.

And it is a wonder someone actually made a modern Hawaiian surf-themed restaurant chain. There is the original Duke's in Waikiki, one in Malibu, one in La Jolla, and here in Huntington Beach. Very bad taste and I don't mean décor. I am a massive fan of tiki kitsch and faux koa wood, but Hawaiian food—that's what surprises me. That someone made a chain of up(ish)scale restaurants that serves Hawaiian cuisine.

Duke's doesn't actually serve "real" Hawaiian cuisine, I suppose. Real Hawaiian cuisine is Spam musubi, a thick slice of marinated Spam laid on a ball of sushi rice and tied down with some seaweed. And macaroni salad with extra Miracle Whip. And heaping balls of totally flavorless white rice.

The restaurant is named after Duke Kahanamoku. He had very fine bone structure, an enviable head of hair, an Olympic gold medal, a bevvy of Hollywood starlets, and is credited with re-gifting surfing to the world.

Surfing had gone to Polynesia and flowered mostly in Hawaii, but then the white man came. First Captain Cook in 1779, who watched the Hawaiians dance upon the waves. They killed him by smashing the back of his head in for disrespecting their island, but white men are a virus and soon more came and more and more. They brought a nasty work ethic, exotic diseases, and a Calvinistic outlook that judged surfing to be a gross pastime. And so it was discouraged along with other quintessentially Hawaiian things and the native population went into severe decline, dying from disease, being worked to death, being completely displaced by modern savagery.

The tide began to turn, slightly, at the turn of the century. America's wealthy had discovered Hawaii as the perfect vacation spot and were soon steaming across the Pacific to newly built hotels on Waikiki's almost perfect sand, and these tourists fell in love with Hawaiiana. Coconut drinks, frangipani necklaces, hula, surfing.

Duke Kahanamoku was born a pureblooded Hawaiian in 1890 and came of age during this slow shift from Hawaii being a sort of indentured-servant Calvinist hell to a coconut-scented paradise. A high school dropout and one of five brothers, he would spend his days playing on the beach, swimming and surfing. Most of the Hawaiians at the time would ride shorter boards in the smaller waves nearer shore. Kahanamoku fashioned himself a traditional *olo*, what the Hawaiian royalty once rode, and caught bigger waves far out to sea. As he approached shore, he would twirl around or stand on his head and the mainland tourists would thrill at this display.

It was such a wonderful novelty to behold. Such strange fun for visitors to watch, but there was no real place for surfing in society. And so it was swimming that first made Duke Kahanamoku famous. He broke the American records in the fifty- and hundred-yard distances and won a gold medal at the 1912 Summer Olympics in Stockholm.

After achieving renown, Duke went on a publicity run to America's east coast and brought surfing with him, wowing the large crowds that gathered before ending up in sunny Southern California. By the 1920s, the worm had officially turned and surfing had been re-reborn in twentieth-century America.

I don't really know why those very early tourists who came to Hawaii didn't want to try surfing for themselves as they sat on the Royal Hawaiian's shaded veranda sipping mai tais, eating whatever it was that people ate there before Spam and watching those beach boys ride Waikiki like they do today. I don't know why it had to travel across the sea to colder water and worse waves to fully become a poison. But there they sat sipping, eating, and passively watching—with one notable exception.

The great Samuel Langhorne Clemens, better known as Mark Twain, wrote of his 1872 experience:

In one place we came upon a large company of naked natives, of both sexes and all ages, amusing themselves with the national pastime of surf-bathing. Each heathen would paddle three or four hundred yards out to sea (taking a short board with him), then face the shore and wait for a particularly prodigious billow to come along; at the right moment he would fling his board upon its foamy crest and himself upon the board, and here he would come whizzing by like a bombshell! It did not seem that a lightning express train could shoot along at a more hair-lifting speed. I tried surf-bathing once, subsequently, but made a failure of it. I got the board placed right, and at the right moment, too; but missed the connection myself. The board struck the shore in three-quarters of a second, without any cargo, and I struck the bottom about the same time, with a couple of barrels of water in me. None but the natives ever master the art of surf-bathing thoroughly.

Maybe it is strange that an elderly man sporting a wild, bushy moustache and spotless white suit would be the one to jump off the shaded veranda and into the sea. Maybe it doesn't fit a traditional narrative, but traditional narratives fall away when romance is introduced, and Mark Twain's surf froth makes perfect sense in this light because The Great American Novelist had a surf-esque life plan before writing *The Adventures of Tom Sawyer*, *The Adventures of Huckleberry Finn*,

A Connecticut Yankee in King Arthur's Court, and so on. He surfed, yes, but was also thinking about becoming a cocaine baron.

In a 1910 essay, "The Turning Point of My Life", he wrote about a strange traveler he'd met:

Also, he told an astonishing tale about COCA, a vegetable product of miraculous powers, asserting that it was so nourishing and so strength-giving that the native of the mountains of the Madeira region would tramp up hill and down all day on a pinch of powdered coca and require no other sustenance.

I was fired with a longing to ascend the Amazon. Also with a longing to open up a trade in coca with all the world. During months I dreamed that dream, and tried to contrive ways to get to Para and spring that splendid enterprise upon an unsuspecting planet. But all in vain. A person may PLAN as much as he wants to, but nothing of consequence is likely to come of it until the magician CIRCUMSTANCE steps in and takes the matter off his hands. At last Circumstance came to my help. It was in this way. Circumstance, to help or hurt another man, made him lose a fifty-dollar bill in the street; and to help or hurt me, made me find it. I advertised the find, and left for the Amazon the same day.

This was another turning-point, another link. Could Circumstance have ordered another dweller in that town to go to the Amazon and open up a world-trade in coca on a fifty-dollar basis and been obeyed? No, I was the only one. There were other fools there—shoals and shoals of them—but they were not of my kind. I was the only one of my kind.

Except he wasn't the only one of his kind. He was part of a proud and ancient line of surfing coca eaters that stretched away from him into a murky past and away from him into an equally murky future.

"Look at that Billabonic guy getting covered by the wave. What do they call it? Barrel? Look at him barrel…" The Buckeye is nudging his wife and pointing toward a television hung near a fake thatched roof. She gives a passive nod and takes a sip of her mai tai. A replay of the Pipeline Pro surf contest is being shown and the surfer doing barrel is not actually a Billabonic guy but North Shore standout Jamie O'Brien, who is sponsored by Red Bull and Body Glove. He is wearing a Billabong singlet, though, like everyone else in the contest, because the event's title sponsor is Billabong. The same Billabong that just released an Andy Warhol collection.

I once came into Duke's with Jamie's amazing filmer, a friendly boy with the warmest smile named Big Island Damo. He had grown up on Hawaii's Big Island and never left until traveling to Oahu as an eighteen-year-old to film Jamie. And the first time he had ever left the islands was when he came here to Huntington Beach. Big Island Damo had a wonderful lisp and the excitement of a child. Everything he saw was more spectacular than his mind could hold. Trains, giant freeways, people actually moving faster than molasses. The contiguous forty-eight were a wonderland. A kingdom of endless fascination.

When he first went to the beach in Huntington, he was shocked by how many *haoles* lay on the sand, "haole" being the sometimes cute Hawaiian pejorative for white people.

"Brah," Big Island Damo exclaimed. "There'th haole-th everywhere!" When a Primo beer truck passed us, he almost lost his mind. "BRAH! THERETH OUR KING! ON THE TRUCK!" Primo is Hawaii's beer and uses an image of King Kamehameha for their advertising. He was thrilled that Huntington had its own Duke's, but when we went to the Barefoot Bar he was politely asked to please put shoes on. I think in that moment the wonder of America fell away, conceding to a resounding confusion most Hawaiians feel from birth.

I pull out my phone and think about writing a story on how *Surfer* magazine has just stolen *Surfing Magazine*'s Instagram account and turned it into @surferfilms in clear violation of ethics instead. When drinking, I think all of my ideas are amazing and funny, like the ones I used to bring to *Surfing Magazine*. Like Mitt Romney's hair. I'll text them to my best Australian pal and biz partner and he'll post them. In the cold light of sobriety, they are always awful, filled with malapropos and misspellings.

But I've had two mai tais already so dive right in to "Lame: Surfer mag steals shit!"

Buckeye's wife has finished her mai tai and just ordered a Diet Coke and vodka and I don't know that I've ever heard of a grosser combination. I suppose it makes sense, though, in a restaurant featuring the culinary instincts of a culture that combined sushi and Spam. Buckeye doesn't notice. He is staring at the TV, mesmerized, watching newly minted world champ John John Florence snag an even deeper tube than Jamie O'Brien.

"I tell you," he says to no one. "I've never seen more barrel. These Billabonic guys can really surf." John John is sponsored by Hurley and Vans. I watch the bartender fumbling with a can of Diet Coke while watching John John's strange smile on the TV while thinking about surf magazines fighting over Instagram. And cocaine.

The new miracle was infused into beverages, solutions, tonics. A popular early iteration was the coca wine. Coca leaves or purified cocaine distilled in red wine. Abraham Lincoln paid fifty cents for a bottle of Cocaine in 1860, becoming the first person in the United States, apparently, to partake. Ulysses S. Grant was diagnosed with throat cancer and fed cocaine by none other than Mark Twain, who was trying to ease his pain and keep him alive long enough to steal his memories, fractured as they might be, for a book on America's Civil War. Jules Verne drank so much coca wine while writing *Twenty Thousand Leagues Under the Sea* that he felt he was going to live forever and Sir Arthur Conan Doyle, creator of Sherlock Holmes, had the world's most famous detective use cocaine in order "to escape from the dull routine of existence."

Coca-Cola, and its later, grosser, Diet Coke, made the scientific wonder an American brand. Before it was called Coca-Cola, it was called Peruvian Wine Cola. The only remnant of "Peru" that remains in our modern Coca-Cola, and its bastard Diet Coca-Cola, is its red-and-white motif, a nod toward Peru's flag.

In 1900, pure cocaine was selling in the United States of America for twenty-five cents a gram and could be purchased in any store without a prescription. Any pharmacy. According to professor of history of medicine at Yale University David F. Musto in his *Scientific American* story titled "Opium, Cocaine, and Marijuana in American History," Parke-Davis, one of America's oldest drug makers, sold cocaine by telling customers that it "can supply [sic] the place of food, make the

65

coward brave, the silent eloquent and…render the sufferer insensitive to pain." Apparently forgetting to note that it can also render the sufferer insensitive to self-modulation or reflection. And also give the sufferer an ability to solve complex international crises in a single conversation.

It truly was a gilded age, with Americans turning out and turning on. The earliest jazz danced on a bold (toxic) industrialized wind, cocaine was literally everywhere, and surfing had just been dubbed "The Sport of Kings" by none other than turn-of-the-century celebrity Jack London.

The author of survivalist classics *Call of the Wild* and *White Fang* had become famous for his gorgeously descriptive novels, but also for his outsized personality and adventurous spirit. In 1906 he designed a ketch and sailed it from San Francisco to Honolulu. It was there, perched on the grass of the Moana Hotel, that he looked up and:

Suddenly, out there where a big smoker lifts skyward, rising like a sea-god out of the welter of spume and churning white, on the giddy, toppling, overhanging and downfalling, precarious crest appears the dark head of a man. Swiftly he rises through the rushing white. His black shoulders, his chest, his loins, his limbs—all is abruptly projected on one's vision. Where but the moment before was only the wide desolation and invincible roar, is now a man, erect, full-statured, not struggling frantically in the wild movement, not buried and crushed and buffeted by those mighty monsters, but standing above them all, calm and superb.

Like Mark Twain almost forty years prior, London had to give this strange dance a go. Unlike Twain, he was undaunted with his first rough experience and kept at it with the help of legends Alexander Hume Ford and George Freeth. Hume, a South Carolina transplant who had just moved to the islands and become completely addicted to surfing, watched London struggle in the shore break on a too-small board, marched up and told him that he was going to die if he didn't get a longer board.

London followed him and Freeth the next day out beyond the shore break to where real waves bounced and "fought a battle in which mighty blows were struck, on one side, and in which cunning was used on the other side" before finally catching a wave and experiencing what he described as "ecstatic bliss."

And he was hooked, staying out in the water for so long that he became horribly sunburned. But did he care? No. So blistered he could not even move, he sat in bed and wrote, *"But tomorrow, ah, tomorrow, I shall be out in that wonderful water, and I shall come in standing up, even as Ford and Freeth. And if I fail tomorrow, I shall do it the next day, or the next. Upon one thing I am resolved: the Snark shall not sail from Honolulu until I, too, wing my heels with the swiftness of the sea, and become a sunburned, skin-peeling Mercury."*

It is certain that Jack London would have grown his own pterygia had he not been forced back to the mainland, but surfing stayed with him, and his article "A Royal Sport" romanticized surfing for millions of readers enjoying their magazines with a thimbleful of twenty-five-cent cocaine.

And then another thimbleful of twenty-five-cent cocaine.

And then another thimbleful of twenty-five-cent cocaine.

And then another thimbleful of twenty-five-cent cocaine.

Or maybe only the doctors and dentists were reading London with coke-addled eyes. This was the first class of people known to take the miracle of cocaine a bit too far and were dubbed "cocainomaniacs" by the press, who wrote stories about their degenerate behaviors which, in turn, caused a drop in national cocaine consumption by up to half.

It was not until stories of African Americans' abuses, though, that politicians began to devise ways to curb cocaine production and use. At the time, most of America's cocaine was coming from Peru, up through the Panama Canal and to New Orleans. Journalists began to flood newspapers with tales of wild coke-fueled fights and insurrections by predominantly African American dockworkers. Tales of attacks on white Southern women being "the direct result of a cocaine-crazed Negro brain" and America's first drug tsar, Dr. Hamilton Wright, alleged that drugs made African American men uncontrollable and encouraged them to rebel against white people.

Panicked Southerners led to the passage of the United States Pure Food and Drug Act of 1906, which knocked the coca out of Coca-Cola, and then the Harrison Narcotics Tax Act of 1914, which, quite basically, made cocaine, opium, and future derivatives illegal. Cocaine no longer represented the glamorous perfection of scientific knowledge. It was seen as deviant. As decadent. As a naughty mark on the human soul.

And surfing? Surfing was right behind her lover, descending into the realm of depravity. The hole of lusty delight. The pit of sensual despondency. After Jack London had pushed off in his gloriously named *Snark* and written about the dignified royal pastime, crowds began to throng to Waikiki's perfect sands and want it all for themselves. The palms, the coconuts, the warmth and the waves. And a handful of locals who came to be known as "beach boys" were there to cater to their every whim. Loose, charming, drunk and drugged, these Peter Pans would show the tourists hula, cook them a luau, and paddle them around in the shadow of Diamond Head in either canoe or on surfboard.

And that is what turned them on. These beach boys were surfers above all and would surf with tourists and surf without them too, forming a locals' only club called "Hui Nalu," or in English, "wave sliders." They were out on every swell putting on a show for others or just for themselves. Addicted to the big smokers, or as the surf historian Matt Warshaw writes in his History of Surfing, "Surfing was as important to these barefoot troubadours as their sexed-up, easygoing, empty-pocket deviancy. By combining the two, beach boys laid a foundation for what would later be called the surfing lifestyle."

The surfing lifestyle. And I feel my phone buzz in my pocket. I know it is my wife and I know I should have just gone home instead of coming to Duke's and mocking myself. I pull it out ready to catch hell, but it is not my wife. It is the surf filmmaker I was supposed to meet and his text reads, "Chas! So sorry! I totally forgot we have a little premiere thing at the Roosevelt tonight. Come up!"

My wife is going to kill me.

6

The Meeting with the Goddess!

I plod from Huntington to Hollywood in a standard blur. Stop. Go. Speed. Flip off. Make angry face. Change lanes. Listen to a new track by ex-One Direction heartthrob Harry Styles. Listen to a new track by Miley Cyrus's younger sister, Noah. I always listen to the worst music when I'm driving. And writing. I would try and blame my wife's daughter, and some of it is her fault, but it's mostly mine. My heart beats to teenage girl music.

I finally pull into the valet stand at the Roosevelt, which is jammed. I step out of my car to see what's happening and watch a valet who is looking at another valet who is looking at a rented white Jeep Compass who then looks over to me. The front bumper is halfway off and there is a giant dent in the passenger's side door and the whole thing is covered in red mud but I don't know why the valets care. They didn't do it. And this is the damned Roosevelt, not the Chateau Marmont for crying out loud.

I can't remember how many surf parties I've been to here. Definitely more than ten. Maybe even twenty. There is something between the surf industry and the Roosevelt. Some deep and abiding bond. All the brands from Globe to Volcom to Quiksilver to Billabong, even small ones like RadGnar and Let's Party, have thrown something or another here. Movie premieres, product launches, birthday parties, photo exhibitions, promotion fetes, even one celebrating the firing of a team manager. Tonight the surf industry is celebrating the release of a new surf clip by the surf film director I was supposed to be meeting at Duke's and who is supposed to be promoting a new high-top shoe that may or may not be stylish.

When there is no official brand event or party, surfers will still stay here if whatever they're attending is within a twenty-mile radius or even thirty. I don't know that any other Los Angeles hotel is even considered. I don't even know if surfers know the name of another hotel but they all know the Roosevelt and even know how to get here without using Google Maps. It is their true north.

Maybe it is Teddy's?

The once hot Roosevelt lobby club, with its perpetually lusty orange glow and crowds craning necks to see if someone cooler were lurking in neighboring human knots, hosted the best of Hollywood's brightest for a handful of years in the mid-2000s. Meg Ryan, early Paris Hilton, that one guy who wrestled professionally, River Phoenix, Johnny Depp, etc.

The club was started by Amanda Scheer Demme, widow of Ted Demme, who is in her own right a famous photographer and takes the best celebrity pictures ever. All moody and sexy and dark. She took a picture of Joaquin Phoenix, River's brother, smoking a cigarette and getting punched, which wowed. She also took a picture of Travis Fimmel with his perfect nose and his bluest eyes and fuck him. I'm sorry. That is the jealousy writing.

Ted, her departed husband, was a popular figure and talented artist in his own right. He directed the best cocaine film ever starring Johnny Depp. *Blow* was based on the memoir of George Jung who helped the Medellín cartel supply 85 percent of the United States' supply in the 1970s and 1980s. Ted died of a cocaine-induced heart attack in 2002, Amanda made the club in his honor and now, I suppose, surf and the Roosevelt make perfect sense. A deep and abiding bond. A love affair that hides in the orange glow and the memory of neck-craning knots.

I hear the valet ask the Jeep's driver, who I recognize as a professional surfer who rides for RVCA, "Uhhhh are you guys checking in or..."

but he doesn't respond because he is telling his surfer bro, who rides for Rusty, a story about one of his bros who got bottled on the Gold Coast last week.

"So my mate was out surfing Snapper, I guess, and stuffed this guy pretty good. Anyhow, that night outside the Coolangatta Hotel he was drinking a beer and the guy he stuffed came up to him and tried to bottle him. Like there on the sidewalk. The bogan was so drunk though that he just swung and ended up hitting a parked car and passing out on the ground."

I feel bad for the valets because long ago I used to be one, and I shout to RVCA, "Hey! Are you guys staying here?"

He looks up and laughs, "Chas—howzit, mate? Yeah, for two nights."

The valet stutters, slightly, and responds, "Do you have a reservation yet? You have to have reservations because we are expecting a full…"

The two surfers don't let him finish and walk off giggling and reenacting the bottling without taking their ticket. The two valets are left with an uncomfortable conundrum on their hands and look at me but I just shrug and walk toward the door too without my ticket, wondering how quickly I can leave and also wondering if there are more bottling incidents among surfers than any other population grouping.

I had no idea what a "bottling" was prior to heading to Australia's Gold Coast over a decade ago. I was covering the first surf contest of the year, the Quiksilver Pro, and at a pub when I saw some drunken surfer grab a beer bottle, smash it on a table, then wave it in the face of another drunken surfer. Viciously. Manically. It felt like the Wild West and I imagined I was witnessing some odd occurrence but was later told bottlings are so common that the government recently passed a law where glass would not be used after midnight in order to try and curb incidents.

Or maybe it is just an Australian surfer thing. I don't recall ever seeing a bottling in…oh, I take that back. I saw a Brazilian surfer think about bottling a Californian surfer in San Clemente but he couldn't break the bottle and got tackled to the ground first. Fucking surfers. And I hate drinking out of plastic, but I think it is all they use at the Roosevelt and I should probably be happy.

Inside, brand managers, team managers, executive vice presidents, and professional surfers are mingling with an odd assortment of young professionals and computer programmers who think the Roosevelt is still a place to be and accidentally got caught in the surf industry's maw.

A giant movie screen is stretched out over the shallow end of the pool and is flickering with images from a pool party. Bikini-clad girls jumping onto giant blowup donuts in slow motion and splashing each other. A display case featuring the high-tops has been set up near the deep end. I wander over to it and study but still can't tell if they are any good. If the toe is right, if the height is appropriate, if the materials match the ethos of—

I can't tell what the ethos is supposed to be. Brooklyn hipster meets...Bondi hipster or maybe Byron hipster? And is the surfer supposed to wear them at the Roosevelt?

"Chaaaaas..." a voice says behind me in classic upper-register-vowel-extended surf drawl, interrupting my surf journalism. I turn around and see a rep for Grapes the Cat, a surf-branded phone charger that began as an invite-only Instagram account featuring naked girls that got shut down. I don't exactly know how the one attaches to the other attaches to the other, narratively, but it clearly doesn't matter. He is tall with a lantern jaw and jaunty Salty Crew hat. "Howzit, brah?" he says semi-ironically. "You going to Agenda tomorrow?" Agenda is one of the industry trade shows that happens every year, or maybe two times a year, in Long Beach.

"Ho, brah," I respond semi-ironically and tell him, "shoots."

He nods slowly while throwing a semi-ironic shaka. Hawaiian pidgin from the "howzit" to the "ho" to the "brah" to the "shoots" to the shaka are such a part of surf culture that they are used semi-ironically by everyone not Hawaiian. Ironically because making gentle fun of surf and surf culture is the dialect of the industry. Semi because we are all genuinely shallow and can't figure out another way to communicate. I'm even unsure of some of their real meanings. Like shoots. I don't know if shoots means "yes" or "cool" and so I use it interchangeably for both yet have never been corrected.

And while he is throwing his semi-ironic shaka, he accidentally knocks a lower-tier Hollywood writer-type's cocktail out of his hand. It bounces off the pool deck since it is damned plastic. The writer looks down at his polo shirt, which caught some of his cocktail, and then at Grapes the Cat, and then at me. It seems like he is going to say something but his eyes go wide for one split second before he shakes his head and retreats into the crowd.

His wide eyes displayed a touch of fear. Only the smallest touch, but it was still there, and it is a wonder that surf still retains a whiff of danger. A smell of brawling danger. On the inside it feels so conservative. So stiff. So Orange County scrubbed. So tight. So paranoid. But when surf touches real life it becomes apparent that, externally, the perception differs. Young professionals and computer programmers and maybe even lower-tier Hollywood writer-types think surfers are unhinged. No-goods. Bad seeds. And maybe they're right.

It was Honolulu's beach boys that set the narrative tone in the 1920s with their empty-pocket sexed-up deviancy and it translated perfectly to Depression-era California. Jobs were scarce already, but surfing had just taken root and waves didn't cost a dime. Surfers would stay on the beach all day and some would stay on the beach all night. Drinking, lighting fires, surfing, living on what were then the absolute fringes of society.

There is a classic story of a 1930s legend named Gene "Tarzan" Smith who lived in a cave that he carved out of the sandstone near Orange County's Corona del Mar. He was a drunk and a fighter and on weekends would paddle his surfboard across the Newport Harbor, dance in the Rendezvous Ballroom, get drunk, get in fights, then paddle back to his cave at night. He could paddle so well that he once made it all the way from Oahu to Kauai, a seventy-mile journey that took thirty hours. It is said that by the end of it Tarzan thought he was paddling up Hollywood Boulevard, which makes perfect sense seeing that the Roosevelt sits at the corner of Hollywood and Orange.

Not all surfers were derelicts, of course, but I'll be damned if the general embryonic future surf culture instinct didn't lean heavily toward the black, even if accidentally. Up until the 1930s, for example, if you wanted to surf you had to carve your own board from a tree. There was no such thing as a commercially produced surfboard. But then the Great Depression happened and the son of a manufactured home company magnate decided his life was going to be poor hell no matter what he did, so he dropped out of Stanford and convinced his father to let the company let him carve surfboards. He had been to the beaches and seen the future.

His father agreed, and in 1932 young Myers Butte started pumping Swastika Surfboards out of the Pacific Systems Homes warehouse. Yes. Swastika. According to *The History of Surfing*, "Butte knew the normal hand-carved seventy-pound surfboard was too heavy so he made wholesale buys on light kiln-dried balsawood. The boards had a balsa core and redwood on the sides, nose and tail. Half-inch strips of redwood or mahogany might also be laid along the board's vertical axis. The laminated mixed-wood designs were nearly as strong as the one-piece hand-carved redwoods, but much lighter—a ten-foot Swastika weighed just forty-five pounds—and each board, with its contrasting and perfectly interlocked pieces, looked as if it had been pulled from Frank Lloyd Wright's sketch pad."

Each was fire-emblazoned with the hook-crossed design later made famous by Adolf Hitler. A cartoon surfer who even looked strikingly like Adolf Hitler was used as Swastika's first advertisement. There he stood proud above the waves. Very face forward. Very strong bone structure and combed hair. Very Leni Riefenstahl. Very Aryan with the shadow of his upper lip forming what looked like a small toothbrush moustache. And even though Nazi Germany wasn't a "thing" in 1930, surfers are prescient sons of bitches, the future somehow reflecting in the shallow pool of their souls.

I refocus on what Grapes the Cat is saying and think it involves how their Agenda booth is going to feature some girls who just left Monster Energy and are starting their own modeling thing. I am going to ask him if anyone has actually ever tried Monster Energy drink and if anyone actually thinks the Monster Girls are hot but am interrupted by a kinetic ball of fire asking if either us know where to get some toot. "Toot" sounds like it might also be Hawaiian pidgin but is actually the favorite Australianism for cocaine. He is drunk enough to be completely unbothered by the stigma of asking directly and also a filmer—the most sunburned class of the surf industry hierarchy. The most put upon and the least celebrated. They have to sit for hours in the boiling sun pointing cameras at professional surfers who spin in the distance and what the hell sort of job is that? I mean, clearly more understandable than surf journalist or surf historian, but neither Matt Warshaw nor I have to sit in the boiling sun. Matt Warshaw doesn't even have the opportunity to see the boiling sun. He lives in Seattle. I tell the filmer that I don't have any toot and look over at Grapes the Cat, who is stuttering an excuse, but the filmer has already seen a better possible mark and has skipped off toward the pool.

The conversation returns to Agenda and some rumor swirling about two middle-aged Australians who are buying up surf properties for way more than they are worth. They bought a removable fin company, a wave forecasting website, and a fake version of *BeachGrit* called *Stab*. Spending impulsively and wildly but also fighting a lot, apparently. And while I just told Grapes the Cat "shoots" when he asked me if I was going to Agenda, I was totally lying. Or maybe lying, since I still don't know exactly what it means and how it is used. But now I know that I have to go. Impulsive wild-fighting Australians? There is only one thing that can mean.

Love. And my thread.

7

Sacred Marriage!

I drive to Long Beach early after getting home way too late from Hollywood. Tiredness swells in me. Apathy. I am so apathetic that when Drake comes on the radio I don't switch the station and I hate Drake. Like *hate* hate Drake. Like, really. And now there is a strange cover of Sublime's "Santeria" bouncing between the cavernous walls of the Long Beach Convention Center or maybe it actually is Sublime and I hate that I actually came to Agenda almost as much as I hate Drake.

The Monster Girl standing in front of What Youth's booth is trying to explain to me the mechanics of a T-shirt gun. The high-powered cannon that hype men and women use to rocket tight-necked T-shirts into adoring audiences and that Monster Girls use to shoot ten-year-old surf fans in the face during Huntington Beach's US Open of Surfing with fluorescent green garbage.

"I dunno, you just have to put it in there and then the pressure builds and then it just pops," she says while making a rubbing up-and-down motion with her hand. It all reads very sexual here in print, and would theoretically look seductive, but in person it is not because have you ever caught a T-shirt from a howitzer? Even accidentally? There is, first, a painful realization that stings from hand to elbow followed quickly by a painful realization, when unfurled, that the T-shirt's neck would choke a very small baby and will definitely choke you no matter how unfashionably you prefer your T-shirts.

I have never understood why cannon fodder T-shirt necks have to be so tight. Are they cheaper to produce? Do the market analyses point to trending tight necks? Do tight-necked T-shirts have better aerodynamics when rolled into the shape of a bullet or are the Chinese trying to choke a certain percentage of the population to death before a full-scale invasion?

I don't know and the Monster Girl doesn't care. Her demonstration is over and her bored smoky eyes are scanning over my shoulder, taking in the crowd, gauging potential for after-parties, looking for friends, waiting for the minutes to tick by before she is sent packing to Riverside. I wonder how long her shift will be as I untether and drift back into the sea of flannel shirts, beanies, black jeans, and Vans and shuffle aimlessly.

I wonder if she was once excited to be a Monster Girl. Like, if that was once her dream.

The booths—Billabong, Rip Curl, RVCA, Banks, Brixton, Captain Fin, Deus, Huf, Rusty, The Critical Slide Society—all look like a version of the same thing. Like a tricolored mural of the five-year apocalypse. Of the dizzying fall. Design that hasn't changed for multiple seasons. Everyone still stuck on anchor motifs and hipster minimalism except without the attention paid to fit. Glum brand ambassadors filling the odd order for even glummer retailers. Glummer retailers wondering if fortune will ever smile upon them again. If the kids will ever lust for a surf label again. If Zara is hiring.

The rumor of the two middle-aged Australians on a surf-buying spree is just that. Rumor. They are not here, though I do see a friend who met with one of them last week. He says, "Oh, man, he was so bad. He was wearing boot-cut jeans and, like, had a big watch."

The only booth that is noticeably different is Quiksilver's. That brand once threw parties that rivaled the best of Hollywood. Parties in Paris's Grand Palais. Parties that featured waves of bottomless Veuve and mountains of caviar and mountains of cocaine except the cocaine was not expressly supplied or at least that's how I've heard it told.

The smart businessman, though, smells surfers from a mile away and when surfers are in town knows to strike with as much product as he can find. For Quiksilver's fortieth anniversary Grand Palais party, smart businessmen from as far away as Transylvania were waiting outside with pockets full of gear. But maybe the Transylvanians were simply there because the party featured Tony Hawk who really and truly looks like the walking dead.

Quiksilver once rented half of Agenda's tradeshow floor and filled it with the glitter and hope and their multibillion-dollar valuation. The first brand in all of surf to reach that glorious height. Now bankruptcy has relegated them to a dark corner where hastily screen-printed T-shirts are staple-gunned to a prefabricated wall. Rubberneckers shuffle past just to take it in, but none make eye contact with the remaining Quiksilver employee lest whichever brand they work for is next. Lest they are next staple-gunning the tatters of a once sunny "surf career" to a prefabricated wall.

I shuffle past with the rest of the rubberneckers except the new surf journalist beat of my cursed heart forces my head up and my eyes forward. To pass and not take it in would be like Woodward and Bernstein refusing to look Nixon directly in his green eye. Like Edward R. Murrow failing to fully examine Joseph McCarthy's motives. Like Megyn Kelly wilting under Donald J. Trump's menacing stare and sexist growl. To turn away from the stink of the time. So I look and take it in, ready to cringe but actually liking the retro hot pink cartoon scribble dog saying, "Stay Fucking High!" in a cartoon bubble on a tattered sweatshirt also featuring Quiksilver's iconic mountain and wave logo. It feels like they mean it and so there is some genuine angsty pop and wonder if there would be some amazingly lucid revelation from the remaining Quiksilver employee, some pearl of wisdom only gleaned after fasting forty days and forty nights, but I'm neither Woodward nor Bernstein nor Murrow nor Kelly and I don't feel like talking about a bummer while looking for love, so I shuffle on.

Past Nixon, Oakley, O'Neill, Hurley, Body Glove, Vissla, D'Blanc who may not be bankrupt but are also totally and completely uninspired. "Surf style" has become so concretely uniform with brand managers turning to trend forecasters in order to stave off death so everything feels the exact same. Anchors and bullshit. Anchors pulling all this bullshit to the ocean's floor. And then I stumble upon an oasis of cynical joy sitting where a booth should be but didn't get constructed. A surf filmmaker, two professional surfers, and a team manager who have just launched a surf traction company named Octopus. There is absolutely no money in surf traction. No margin, no volume, no nothing. The average surfer probably spends thirty-five dollars on surf traction a year. No more. Probably less. And no non-surfer touches the stuff. Why would they? To stick weird shapes on walls? To, umm, use it in kinky sex dungeons? But these four started it for exactly that reason. "Everyone was so worried about the bottom line and making money, but this is surfing," the surf filmmaker told me right before the launch. "It's all totally absurd. We just want to have fun again. It's literally surfing. Can you even think of anything more absurd to monetize?"

And even in the midst of the five-year apocalypse with no end in sight, surf still produces rebels and this thread extends back four thousand years. From the surfers who start impossible to monetize companies to the Peruvian fisherman rebelling against his bleak surroundings by putting his feet up on the handlebars. The Hawaiian king rebelling against the pressure of his plebeian bone-crushing existence by rolling on the waves, to the Hawaiian plebe rebelling against his bone-crushing king by surfing too, to the early prewar Californian rebelling against taste by paddling in relatively freezing cold water, living in sandstone caves, riding Swastikas, to the postwar Californian rebelling by trespassing past Malibu's "Keep Out!" sign while creating the boldest counterpoint, to baby boom hegemony and rocking the rest of the modern time. Or at least rocking the rest of my modern time.

Malibu. The word sounds good, it feels good, but it wasn't always good or at least accessible. It is a Spanish bastardization of the native Chumash "Hamaliwu," which means "Loud Waters." There was a small village there where fishermen would push up the river and out to sea. The Spanish coopted the land from the Chumash and broke it into a 13,300-acre named Rancho Malibu. The Americans coopted it from the Spanish after the US-Mexican War with the cocaine fiend Ulysses S. Grant writing the last surviving deed when he granted it to an Irishman named Matthew Keller, who sold the whole plot thirty-five years later to Fredrick Hastings Rindge and his wife May K.

It was May K. who tenaciously took on all comers to keep Malibu private. She fought the railroad, she fought the highway commission, she fought the sons of bitches carrying giant wood planks who desired to do unspeakable things to her waves.

The very first surfers who rode Malibu, Sam Reid and Tom Blake, had to park their car two miles away in 1927 and paddle up the coast. It was, I'm certain, as magnificent then as it was now, but the equipment of the time couldn't quite handle its speed and May K. made it a pain in the ass to reach, so it was left alone until Hitler was vanquished and America's boys came streaming home with a taste for blue skies and wide open spaces. With a taste for suburban Southern California.

This postwar explosion, its perpetual sun, tabula rasa, potential for anything because nothing really existed before, transformed Los Angeles from a place of Hollywood dreams to an expansive reality and by the early 1950s the basin rocketed past Chicago as America's second-largest population center. Freeways, cars, palm trees, swimming pools. And while the upstanding new residents went about marrying and booming babies to fill brand-new tract homes, the derelicts shook out to a place where they could ply their deviant trade alone.

And can you imagine a better name than Loud Waters? Than Malibu? It sounds good, it feels good, it feels like a rock n' roll version of a Frank Lloyd Wright sculpture and those Chumash knew everything and we should have never taken their land and a pox on all our houses but also Malibu. Former *Surfer* magazine editor Paul Gross wrote that it "is the exact spot on Earth where ancient surfing became modern surfing." But why exactly Malibu? What makes it different from any other spot?

It begins with the wave and I won't go into its mechanics because there is nothing duller than wave mechanics. Not even Algebra 2.

In short, the way energy pulses from the deep storms of the Pacific and wraps and bends and hits the cobblestone floor and folds over on itself is perfect. Absolutely perfect. But really, the essence of Malibu is the beach. Just like Waikiki, where the beach boys got lusty in the sand—the sexed-up deviants—and Malibu's beach is even better than Waikiki.

Surf historian Matt Warshaw writes, "Malibu wasn't so much a surfing location as it was a small, intimate, well-designed surfing theater." And what a wordsmith, what a ~~Linus~~ Linnaeus and, really, he probably should have finished with his PhD and gone on to do something valuable with his life, making his family proud in the process, but I am glad he didn't. His shallow turn makes me feel slightly better about my own.

The hook of sand that hugs the perfect wave is also the perfect size. Not too big, not too small. Not too near, not too far. Not too hot, not too cold. The wave breaking within spitting distance, that perfect wave, which pushed surfboard design and physical ability into the future but the beach. The beach became a petri dish. Those who congregated here were already rebelling against the heavy cultural push to settle down and make a family. There is no room for career when days are spent idling on the beach. The boys had been to war and now they were on a beach, sun shining, waves peeling, and they were never going to leave. They were surfers.

Up until Malibu in the 1950s, surf had always been married to some other physical expression in order to give it value. It was tied to rowing, life-saving, long-distance paddling, swimming. You did those other things and also surfed and surfing was completely secondary. The postwar boys, though, stripped away the clunky extremities. They needed nothing other than surfing and needed nothing else full stop. Besides trouble, adrenaline, sex, drugs, and booze. Living on the beach is free. Waves are free. The sun is free and surfing is free and also impossible to fit into a normal life anyway, but it was this version of surfing, this rebellion, this addictive consumption, that began mirroring its lover cocaine closer, maybe, than it ever had before even as cocaine itself was slipping further and further into the recesses of history.

The Malibu crowd was a teeming mess of fuckups—man-boys with names like Tubesteak and Da Cat—and they ran the beach like a guttersnipe fiefdom. There were no rules other than the ones they made. No police, no lifeguards, no parents, no authority. They did what they wanted, how they wanted. And by the mid-1950s this freedom was starting to draw. Malibu was getting flooded with urban kids fleeing the new American cult of conformity, but surfing always only belongs to a few and these newcomers.

And the man-boys were mean sons of bitches to these newcomers. Their worldview was "us vs. them" and they would steal, cajole, play pranks, yell, swear, drink, drink, drink, and surf. And surf. And surf. The surfers before had been rebels but not like this new batch, and I think it was precisely because they had set surfing free. Like cocaine freed from the leaf, surfing freed from rowing, life-saving, long-distance paddling, and swimming became potent. Addicting on a whole new scale, churning out junkies who acted like junkies.

Surfers of today can look back on these 1950s Malibu surfers and see Founding Fathers, but they were assholes. Shallow, narcissistic, selfish assholes, and doesn't that just sound familiar? Don't that just feel like Teddy's circa 2001 and the Roosevelt circa two nights ago and Agenda circa right now?

The Octopus boys and I have been joined by a rep for Fox, a motorcycle brand that also does surf trunks, hoodies, and T-shirts for some unknown reason. He is wearing a flat brimmed hat slightly off-center, a Rob Dyrdek DC shirt, black shorts, white socks pulled up to his knees, and a pair of puffy tongued Circa shoes, mocking the mid-1990s inland empire aesthetic. His sendup is so subtle that only the most tuned in would know that he is actively poking fun of his brand's only customer. As self-destructively rebellious as starting a surf traction company in this economic environment. He is a jittery mess right now because he just got texted that Trestles is pumping and not too crowded since the entire surf industry is sitting inside the Long Beach Convention Center.

"Fuck. Fuck! Should I bail? What if I bail?" he keeps uttering as he paces back and forth in front of us in his costume. "Fuck. I'll totally get fired if I bail, but, fuck! Jimmicane said it was solid four foot and, like… fuck…uncrowded!"

Trestles, just south of San Clemente, is modern-day Malibu. It is California's high-performance modern heart with the emphasis on high because this, right here, is what untethered surfing leads to. This. Pacing, ranting, edgy, chatty, perpetually unfulfilled, always hunting. It is an infection. A proper addiction beginning with that first proper wave.

I actually remember mine. It was in Oregon and I was fourteen and Julie Briggs had just broken up with me via note slid through the metal slats on my locker. She was smart and going places. I was a "surfer" because I loved what it meant, what it stood for, even though I had spent the last four years barely standing in the whitewash. But Julie Briggs slipped a note in my locker telling me this wasn't going to work because I was dumb and going nowhere in my life and dumb because I wore Pirate Surf shorts and T&C T-shirts to Marshfield High School every day, even though it was always cold and always raining. I ran all the way home, threw my goofy yellowed seven-foot pintail surfboard in my mom's Grabber Blue Ford Falcon, and she drove me to Bastendorff Beach and I put on my wetsuits and caught a real wave. I mean "real wave." It was some freezing cold reform that had hit a weird sandbar and was actually working, for the first time in accidental history, down the line. Not closing out in typical fashion and maybe as tall as my five-foot head. I put on my hideous diving wetsuit over my holey three-year-old other wetsuit, paddled out wanting to die because Julie Briggs had just broken up with me. Julie Briggs. Redheaded and smart and on her way to an all-girl's college. And I caught one and actually accidentally turned because I no longer feared death and actually accidentally raced down the line.

Raced down that open wave face, a little up, a little down, and was flooded with a sensation that I had never been flooded with before and have never been flooded with in quite the same way again. Where had this been my whole life? And so long Julie Briggs. This first sensation lasted exactly three minutes and I needed it again.

I stayed out in the freezing cold water until the sun went down, my mom shivering on the beach, wondering what the hell had come over me. But surfing had come over me. The addiction. And here is the thing and only a thing that surfers will actually know: The feeling you get from that first wave is the worst thing that ever happens because it is heaven and you chase it forever without replicating. I remember this first wave but I remember none after because the sensation of surfing lasts only as long as the wave does and then you are stuck and then you are chasing it forever from hit to hit to get my nose in the fun dip.

Cocaine might have been a semi-benign historical footnote through the 1950s, but it sure feels to me like surfing kept cocaine alive. It replicated its love's mannerisms, the beat of its heart, until the 1960s flipped the entire world on its head and demanded cocaine's return. Her triumphant reentry. And it was surfers who were there on the ground floor.

Fox decides to bail to surf Trestles. I watch him scamper through the crowd in his 909 costume and chuckle with the rest of the Octopus boys before we turn our attention to the disaster that is Modom. They just made an anti-shark leash, in cooperation with anti-shark company SharkBanz, that apparently shoots out a radio signal, or something, that confuses sharks into not biting. A boy in Florida just got bit while wearing the same technology. Like, his arm almost got bitten off. He was wearing the bracelet version of SharkBanz technology that he got for Christmas and it shouldn't be funny but totally is.

The conversation swings from Modom to the upcoming US Open of Surfing to a funny Hawaiian man who had just lost an arm while driving a car because he had it sticking out the window and it seems as good a time as any to shift back to cocaine so I say, "Lemme hear your best stories," and they all smile coy smiles but no one offers any up. I just transitioned into "that fucking surf journalist" in their eyes. The "fucking dick that everyone hates."

Fucking hell. It is one of the things that drives me the craziest about this ill-begotten life. Surfers think they are the most important people on the planet for some completely unknown reason, languish under the completely mistaken impression that the entire world is just waiting to hear their deepest, darkest secrets. That the entire world is going to lap up my sordid tales of their gilded lives. I know for a *Welcome to Paradise, Now Go to Hell* fact that this is not true. Nobody, and I mean literally no body, gives two shits.

The bad stories, the naughty stories, are the only ones worth sharing, anyhow. Keith Richards isn't shy about his cocaine use. It is what makes him Keith Richards, for crying out loud. So why are surfers so button-lipped about the only thing that makes them remotely interesting?

8

Finding Love
in the Underworld!

I leave Agenda before lunch because I am angry. Also because I don't want to have anything to do with the inevitable taco truck plus Corona Light thing that is bound to happen. But I am mostly angry. Fuck surfers. Fuck their deviant-yet-chickenshit hearts. Fuck their shirking historical greatness. Fuck their silence. And why are they silent? Why don't they all profess their love from the rooftops? Why don't they belt sonnets? If surfers really accept who they are, deep in their hearts, I have no doubt in mine that the surf industry would come roaring back. That the kids would want Volcom and Quiksilver and Billabong and Reef once again. Not because the hangtags would be fitted with little cocaine baggies but because the love story is true and truth resonates. But I have never, in all my days, seen one good representation of surfers and cocai—

And then I suddenly remember: *Sea of Darkness!* A phantom documentary about cocaine and the surf industry, a mirage that detailed a rarely discussed chapter of our history. I met its maker, Michael Oblowitz, almost a decade ago on Oahu. He had been a myth before that. A man who had dared make a movie about the surf industry's direct connection to cocaine and heroin with real surf industry folk, CEOs of companies, brand managers, marketing directors, etc., actually talking on film about it. I didn't believe it. There was no way. The surf industry. The conservative, stiff, so Orange County scrubbed Disney NFL, tight, paranoid surf industry actually copped to it all?

So I tracked him down on the North Shore when I was writing my first godforsaken book. He sat me on the moldy bed of the musty surf shack he was renting while the surf crashed loudly outside, stuck a VHS tape in a machine, turned the volume up way too loud, and pressed play.

And *Sea of Darkness* was the best surf movie I had ever seen. I wrote in that first surf book, "It is about the discovery of G-Land by the surfers and the cocaine and the heroin and the jails and later the founding of Quiksilver. But he only screens it at small festivals and for people he knows. He says it is too heavy to release. Too dangerous. He is worried about the blowback from the industry and more importantly from Hawaiian locals who were, are, involved in the drug trade, and he may be right to be completely paranoid. He is from South Africa and used to make vampire softcore porn for Showtime."

Looking back, my description lacked grace and also I don't think he was or is worried about industry blowback or Hawaiian local blowback, though almost a decade later *Sea of Darkness* is still unreleased. Michael told me after the book had come out, "Bruh, I was paranoid when you were there because I had just done so much coke. Like a ridiculous amount. I'm not afraid of the industry."

But why, then, has it not been released more than a decade after being made? Is there some deeper reason for surfer silence? Something else the powers are trying to hide besides a pretty good time? Thankfully, and maybe not coincidentally, I learned where his office is just a few weeks ago from a handsome French Moroccan, and so I get in my car and drive from Long Beach to Venice, listening to NPR until it transitions to a story about the rise of artificial intelligence being met with mixed reactions at SXSW. I switch to The Chainsmokers' new song and bop along like a teenage girl until I magically find a parking space off Abbott Kinney.

While I feed the meter, a bum yells in my ear about needing five bucks because he just got out of jail and has to get a bus ticket from Venice so he can get to Riverside or Corona or Chino or wherever and visit his grandmother at a nursing home. Every bum in southern California uses a version of the same story. Like some bum screenwriter gave each of them a surefire narrative to spin for fundraising. A very modern, totally-now hero's journey featuring five bucks, jail, the inland empire, and a grandma. To be honest, it is more compelling than Joseph Campbell's work, but only because it is devoid of ego yet filled with an over-the-top bravado. Each bum embraces the role wholly, bringing himself to tears as he talks about both jail and grandma and smiling at how easy it will be for him to solve his problem. Just five bucks!

I give him a buck. He asks, "You got any cigarettes?" When I shake my head, he peels off to perform Act I Scene 1 for an Asian man with a lanyard around his neck. And Venice. Fucking Venice. If Malibu was the exact spot on earth where ancient surfing became modern surfing, then Venice is the exact spot on earth where modern surfing becomes unrecognizable, and it has nothing to do with the bum. His knockoff mythology is the best part of this damned place. Google is the worst part. The web company moved an office here a few years ago into a Frank Gehry-designed thing with huge binoculars out front which might not be the best icon for a group that is sometimes accused of peeking through our digital windows.

It is all the surfboards lined against a ruddy wall that really bothers me, though. Soft tops of various shape and length. Yellowed longboards. Stubby plastic things that only look like surfboards but would never be able to catch a wave. It's like they want their lanyarded employees to paddle out during lunch and make a mockery of the sport of kings and noble Peruvian fishermen. Like they want them to take their pale flesh out into the already very lackluster surf and paddle around with surfboard noses sticking straight in the air and arms and legs wailing uncontrollable and giggling. Like they are purposefully and carefully trying to drain the last vestiges of romance from anything related to wave riding.

Or maybe *The Inertia* is the worst. The exercise/diet/mountain sport website has its offices adjacent to Venice proper and also covers surf since its founder/editor was once the web editor at *Surfer*. Apparently he thought what was missing from the surf media landscape was a *Huffington Post*-esque point-of-viewless take on everything from "Chevrolet's New Bolt EV Might Be the Perfect Eco-Friendly Vehicle for Surfers" to "I Confess I'm a High-Performance Longboarder." And this bullshit purposefully and carefully tries to drain the last vestiges of edge, of danger, of sin, of degradation from anything related to surf journalism. To try and bring some sort of ecological, health-conscious meaning to the utter pointlessness. To maim even more profoundly than any Google employee flopping in Venice's shore break ever could, or to at least maim me.

But right now I don't care. I need to find Michael Oblowitz's office and wander up and down past food trucks and short-sleeved polo tech workers until I remember that his office is in Santa Monica, not Venice, damn navigational amnesia, and go back to my car, this time giving a homeless grandma a buck, thereby cutting the entire arc out of the hero's journey.

I find his 1980s California mistake easily once in the right neighborhood. It feels like Tijuana. Poorly thought out, poorly made. There are no lanyards. There are blacked-out windows and a tiny breezeway. I walk up those stairs feeling slightly disoriented but also hopeful because there is a stench of degradation even though we are miles and miles from Orange County.

Three separate offices front another walkway overlooking Dumpsters, but I find the one he is in because the door is ajar and I hear South African "bruhs" and "fuuks" breezing through its crack. I push in and there he is, standing in the middle of a room filled with black leather recliners and computer screens, wearing a stripped shirt, leather jacket, leather boots, and raw denim like he is some sort of Marlon Brando starring in *The Wild One* waving his arms wildly.

"Everything. The Gibson from nineteen sixty-four, the Telecaster, my collection of Frank Sinatra rings…gone." Michael Oblowitz turns and sees me come through the door and spreads his arms wide. "Chas Smith.

Just in time. You won't believe what happened to me yesterday. Fuuk, bruh. Walk with me. I need a coffee. I have been up all night." He seems agitated but also like he is having the time of his life. Euphoric. Laughing his endearing, smoky, South African rolling laugh. We head back to the walkway, breezeway, down the stairs and onto the street. A bum starts to come over but then thinks again and retreats to a sunny wall.

Michael is a bigger man, as in fatter, but moves with that particular bounce that bigger surfers have. I've paddled out with a couple of kegs who look like they would be lumbering disasters but surfed with the grace of a ballerina. Come to think of it, I've even paddled out with Michael on Oahu's North Shore at a wave called Quonset Huts or something like that. He positively glided, finding perfect trim, moving up and down with subtle efficiency. Like a tiny dancer.

"So fuuk. It started when I was on the North Shore two days ago," he says as we rush along the sidewalk still very upbeat. "I got a call from my partner, my life mate, whatever you want to call her, and she was hysterical. Some thieves had come to the house and bashed out the giant plate-glass window with a sledgehammer. They went inside and trashed the place. Literally trashed the place. The violence, I mean. The violence. It's like they were angry. They took all of her jewelry. Items she will never get back. They took so many of my vintage guitars—" a television writer passes us and looks up, bleary-eyed. Maybe he isn't a television writer, but he is carrying an older MacBook Pro and looks emotionally abused.

We tuck into the small coffee kiosk with unfinished walls and a chalkboard menu. The barista waits for him to finish talking about dead-mom jewelry before asking what he would like. "A Mexican coffee with extra Mexican in it…what makes the Mexican taste? And whatever my friend Chas is having."

I tell her I'm cool because it is ten in the morning and I'm already dreaming about my first cocktail.

"Devastating. But the violence. The rage. It is like they hated us. Here, I have pictures." He fishes his giant iPhone from his pocket and begins flipping through his gallery. I see the smashed plate-glass windows, the empty places where guitars once were, drawers torn out of dressers and thrown on the bed, empty Rolex boxes. "Those are the Rolex boxes, and, uh oh, there is the cocaine." He starts to laugh. "My son Orson went over before the cops arrived and took this picture and said, 'Oh Dad, what should we do about this?' I forgot I even had that. I have no idea how old it is or even where it came from." He is laughing his rolling laugh, and I study the picture closely. It looks like a full kilo brick of coke, like a drug-raid newspaper picture. He flips to the next image before I can ask if it is a kilo or just dressed like a kilo for Halloween. "And here are the boxes of my art and films that I was sending off to the Museum of Modern Art in New York. They are doing a retrospective of my earlier work. Thankfully they didn't get touched, but," and he pauses, chuckling this time, "why do you always tell people that I directed vampire softcore porn for Showtime? I've had films in Cannes, in Sundance. I've won awards. The Museum of Modern Art is doing a retrospective on me." And his chuckle transitions into his laugh again. I laugh too and tell him I don't know and, now that I think about it, it is pretty rude and it's no wonder everyone hates me. "No, no, it's good, bruh," he says. "I like it."

We march back to his office while he sips his Mexican coffee with extra Mexican and tells me that yesterday he was driving from Santa Monica to Hollywood when the wheel on his Ford Bronco came off. "The whole wheel, bruh. Not a flat tire. Not a blowout. The wheel fell all the way off and when I got out to try to put it on, it looked like someone had removed the lug nuts. First thieves violently destroy my home, then my wheel mysteriously falls off? It's like someone is trying to kill me!" And he laughs his deepest laugh yet.

Back up the stairs, through breezeway, past blacked-out windows and into the same office with the black leather recliners and computer screens. Two editors are here now and punching keyboards absentmindedly, apparently editing a new surf film. Neither of them look like surfers, though. One has a baseball cap pulled almost over his eyes and a perma–New York scowl. The other looks friendly but has long black hair pulled into a ponytail and I wonder if they have been gang-pressed off a vampire porn project into the realm of untold emptiness. Both of them look confused as sun and water and pointlessness flicker.

Michael has fired into a new story that I'm not listening to until he asks, "Do you know what Osama bin Laden told George W. Bush when they first spoke after Nine Eleven?"

I don't know and tell him so, but Michael has already motored on.

"He said, 'You may have the watch but we have the time.'"

He pauses to let the profundity sink in and it is profound so I tell him it's amazing before asking him, "Do you know why I'm here?"

He stops suddenly. "No. Why are you here?"

And I ask directly without beating around the bush, without wasting any more time, "Why are surfers so quiet about their cocaine? It is the greatest and oldest love story the world has ever produced. Why do surfers keep it so under wraps? Why are they so paranoid and afraid and unromantic? Why don't they shout it from the rooftops?"

Michael falls back into one of the black leather recliners, bending one leg back in a way that he shouldn't be able too. Exhibiting some of his tiny dancer ability in this non-oceanic realm. The editor with the baseball hat pulled almost over his eyes looks over quickly and I catch his eyes for a minute. They look tortured but blank. Like he is in the middle of some serious brainwashing. A wave dances in slow motion on his screen but there is no surfer.

He opens his mouth without even pausing, like he has been considering this for some time. "It comes down to smuggling. It is because cocaine has value and it comes back to Marx. Value. Cocaine has real value and it is transactional because cocaine's value is mythical and large. Everybody had access to speed in the sixties. Even in the fifties. Take Bob Dylan. Bob Dylan was apparently awake from nineteen sixty-three to sixty-five. He just couldn't sleep because he would go and get injected with speed. JFK, everybody. That's why they were all so skinny, because they would get injections with vitamin B-three and methedrine. It was very accessible and coke was the mystical drug that had disappeared into the underground of undergrounds. It was extremely expensive, nobody even knew about it. Speed, methedrine,

Benzedrine—all of those drugs were simply emulations of cocaine. Cocaine's value, its abstract value, is that it was rare and came from a different part of the world and that made it expensive. Hitler gave speed to all his boys at Stalingrad running around and then the market was flooded with amphetamines. And it was everywhere in World War II. It obliterated that which it was derived from because all it was doing was replicating cocaine. Cocaine just faded away, but I remember reading the first real account of the reemergence of cocaine and it was from John Lennon and Paul McCartney. They were English, of course, so they were snobs, and they had been given by some royal family member this substance that was the preserve of elites and millionaires and billionaires and people like that. So cocaine had this cache, this value-added cache that speed didn't have, and I think that value-added cache is what made it enticing to smuggle because remember, the early surfing travelers were like derelict drug smugglers and we know that from those characters in *Sea of Darkness* but also from these North Shore, Maui, Big Island guys. They accumulated vast wealth, some of them got arrested and some of them didn't, and a pound of cocaine, which was just a small bag, had tremendous value. It was a lot easier to transport than a pound of grass, especially back in the sixties and seventies when drug trafficking prevention policies weren't as sophisticated. You know, they didn't have dogs and they didn't have testing devices or all this stuff, so I think that is where surfing got its re-involvement in cocaine. Surfers could just open a board, fill it up with coke, and make a shit ton of money. More money than they ever even dreamed possible. Smuggling. That's why they keep their mouths shut. Smuggling is surfing's DNA root. There were so many smugglers around that nobody talked about anything. If you spoke about something, they put a bullet in your head. Or worse, they tortured you first, so it was always good to shut up and not talk about it. See no evil, hear no evil."

And for the first time since embarking on this journey, my surf journalist heart soars. Smuggling? I love smuggling! The most romantic profession a man can pursue. Maybe my fascination with illegally sliding goods around originated with *The Dukes of Hazzard*. I remember sitting in Coos Bay as a miserable seven-year-old just months before surfing saved me, watching Bo and Luke Duke smuggle moonshine and thinking, "Fuck the police." And "Yee-haw!" And "Look at them run away from everything. From their miserable racist surroundings. From boredom. Look at them be free."

I consumed every smuggler's tale I could find after that, from Fleming's *Diamonds are Forever* to Hemingway's *To Have and Have Not* to my uncle and his Iran-Contra bootleg of Stinger missiles dressed as medical supplies over the Khyber Pass and into Afghanistan to shoot down Soviet helicopters.

My favorite was Henri de Monfreid's *Smuggling Under Sail in the Red Sea*. That one was the best and detailed how the debonair Frenchman moved hashish from Egypt, or maybe Turkey, to Djibouti. My best friend, Josh, gave it to me recently. After reading we went to Djibouti together and tried to sail a Camper & Nicholson ketch up the Red Sea ourselves but got waylaid by Saudi Arabia, terrorism, antiterrorism legislation, a raging civil war, and a four-foot pirate named Mosquito. It was where I was going to write my aborted masterpiece, *Aljahim,* but at least I got to read Elmore Leonard's *Djibouti* while there and it was another smuggling banger.

I had never really considered smuggling's relationship to cocaine's relationship to surfing and I feel this link, this *ménage à trois*, is exactly what I am looking for. The most romantic thing of all, and sure to be understood by outsiders and celebrated by surfers. I ask Michael if this is why *Sea of Darkness* still hasn't come out, and he goes off on a long tangent about releases and various dull legalities before circling back to Bin Laden. "They have the watch but I have the time."

And he is so exactly right. He has put his finger directly on to one of the greatest shared characteristics in all of surfing. We do keep our mouths shut to protect our treasures. In Coos Bay, when I was surfing those miserable waves, I would hate every other Oregonian surfer I saw. There weren't many, but any I saw I wanted to kill. I wanted to carve nasty messages into their car doors. I wanted them to leave. They were interlopers on my trip. Potential thieves of my waves. And I seethed hatred.

An even better example is Maverick's in Northern California. That wave may be one of the scariest of all. It lurches out of the freezing fog before slamming a rock outcropping and standing straight up to forty, fifty, sometimes sixty feet. Weird kelp and ice-cold water and fog and death. It has claimed multiple lives over the years but was first discovered by a man named Jeff Clark, who was brave enough to paddle out alone and then surfed it alone for over a decade while hungry great white sharks circled beneath his ice-block feet. Any sane person would want at least one buddy on his shoulder to get eaten instead of him.

This is the extent that surfers go to keep their mouths shut. Crowds arrive when lips are loose. And crowds are death. Malibu had reached its own crowded crescendo by the 1960s. The Beach Boys, Elvis Presley, Jan and Dean had all glamorized the surfing lifestyle and who wouldn't want sun, fun, and buns? Surfing was the antidote to postwar dull, such a companion to California's car culture, such a pastel splash to an otherwise black-and-white world that everyone wanted a piece of. The beach was free. The waves were free. All a baby boomer needed was to be there, and so there they went.

And the teeming crowds soon rendered surfing near impossible. Mickey Dora, nicknamed Da Cat, who we met ruling Malibu as a guttersnipe fiefdom alongside Tracy Tubesteak Terry, was the icon of the time. Dark, handsome, mean, he began as a preternaturally talented phenomenon who, courtesy of an abusive but also preternaturally talented surfing stepdad, could bob and weave on a wave like no other. And it was all fun and games, this surfing life, into the 1960s—until Malibu got flooded. Mickey gave one last interview to *Surfer* magazine in the mid-1960s where he said:

"Since November 22, 1963, a curse has fallen upon this country. It has affected us internationally, as well as on the home front. Since this tragic date, the mainland breaks have gradually worsened, and the ground swell has been relegated to the ranks of the unlikely. Cities burn, schools are sieged, and overseas commitments increase. It's only a matter of time before this upheaval shall reach endeavors such as surfing. Monetarily, the manufacturers, publishers, clothes companies, and cinematographers will all collapse, due to overextension, insufficient funds and knowledge, just retribution and nature's cleansing. In short, the creeps who have worked the people over for years are going to fold. The only people to survive this fall will be the true independents, those who will have nothing to do with the upper echelon of this current illusionary prosperity. Any person who complies with the current ruling faction will only provoke his own downfall through corruption and association. People who play ball by reading publications such as this are dooming themselves to extinction."

And that was it. The manufacturers, publishers, and clothes companies didn't even really exist yet. Mickey Dora was simply extrapolating what he saw as possible on Malibu's teeming beaches into the future and surfers, true surfers, understood those words instinctively because they felt them, too. There they went streaming outward, casting flint-eyed glances, away from people, away from a theoretical commoditization searching for empty lines, empty waves, for that first feeling they ever had. That ephemeral first feeling that traced itself through Hawaii to Peru. And thus was born the era of surf travel of an endless summer.

The Endless Summer opened in the summer of 1964 on the surf circuit, one year after Mickey Dora shredded our world, and to substantial crowds. It was so popular, in fact, that it went into wide theatrical release in 1966, highlighting the weird vortex surfing was falling into. Both despising the masses yet attracting more and more and more.

Los Angeles's Bruce Brown filmed Orange County's Robert August and San Diego's Mike Hynson as they set out on a massive adventure, following summer around the globe in search of the perfect, empty wave—something that modern air travel had recently made possible. They packed their bags, their boards, put on the best black suits ever worn on screen, and just left.

Dora has a cameo in the film, even though he had just finished prophesying that "the cinematographers will all collapse." Bruce Brown's perfectly sunny voice narrates the clip as Mickey bobs and weaves though a lineup filled with barneys and kooks. "A surfer who can ride Malibu better than anyone in the world is Mickey Dora. He's very good at winding through the crowds at Malibu without losing any of his composure." The sneer on Mickey's face can be seen draining off the screen, misanthropic rage pouring from his olive skin as he tries to ram the nose of his board into a skinny blonde kid's head.

Bruce, Robert, and Mike found their perfect empty wave, anyhow, at the bottom of the world in Cape St. Francis, South Africa. The scene opens with the little right-hander reeling in the distance while Robert and Mike stand on top of a dune not believing their eyes. There the wave reels and, more importantly, there no one surfs. Empty. Bruce Brown narrates, "and the odds of finding that were ten million to one. The waves looked like they had been made by some kind of machine." While Robert and Mike slide down the dune, ran into the water, and surfed all alone, heads back, hooting and hollering.

When the clip ends, and in a vein of tabula rasa exploration, Brown says, "After we rode Cape St. Francis, we talked to fishermen who come into this area quite frequently and they said the waves were funny-looking things. They looked like pipes. And they said the waves always looked like that, day after day. Same stupid-looking waves." It was the literal dream, except also an illusion created by Brown as he folded the footage of three separate waves then added the boys on the dunes later. Still, the area was near perfect. Surfers just can't help obfuscating. Smoke-throwing bastards.

But the thrown smoke did not matter. The early 1960s saw surf pop. It was the dream. It was a Technicolor mirage with *Beach Blanket Bingo*, *Ride the Wild Surf*, and *Gidget* ramming surf into the mainstream. The early 1960s also saw the United Nations pass the Single Convention on Narcotics and Drugs, thus officially kicking off a worldwide prohibition. Coincidence? Never. Cocaine was, of course, included in the list of substances that everyone from trade unionists to communists to the Birch Society to Republicans to Democrats agreed should be banned outright and criminalized. Some, like heroin and marijuana, entered the parlance of a vibrant yet underfunded counterculture and were ruthlessly policed. Some, like cocaine, became the bastion of sirs, kings, Beatles, and proto-hedge-funders and so the powers that be turned a blind-ish eye.

It was a heavy crackdown on the flood of speed in the early 1960s that gave cocaine its second lease on life. Cheap, easily accessibly amphetamines had ravaged communities, and law enforcement made regulation their number one priority. Cocaine, due to its scarcity and the fact that John Lennon and Paul McCartney were doing it with British nobility, was seen as a luxury product. *Newsweek* likened it to Dom Pérignon in 1977 and *Time* said, "It is the drug of choice for perhaps millions of solid, conventional, and often upwardly mobile citizens." It wasn't a drug. It was an accoutrement. President Gerald Ford's White House issued a study, in 1975, which stated, "Cocaine is not physically addictive, and does not usually result in serious social consequences, such as crime, hospital emergency room admissions or death." President Jimmy Carter's drug policy advisor called cocaine "benign."

All this happy talk about the wonder powder did not change the United Nations Single Convention on Narcotics and Drugs, though, and cocaine's illegality along with its cache opened up a perfect black market. And it seems that derelict surfers just followed their hearts to cocaine's doorstep.

No more than five years after *The Endless Summer* toured America, one year after *Beach Blanket Bingo*, even, places as exotic as Bali were being overrun by surfers looking to find their own Cape St. Francis. There was no industry to support these adventurers, no way to make money off of surfing, and so each would do whatever he could to get by. Still, and as always, living on the beach is free. Waves are free. The sun is free and surfing is free. But the crowds. The crowds are always fucking lame.

Thus it was on Bali that a California surfer by the name of Bill Boyum and a California surfer named Bob Laverty attempted to get away, again, and re-altered surfing's arc. They were part of the first wave, as it were, to launch outward after *The Endless Summer* and surfed Bali's greatest wave, Uluwatu, alone for a few years before the hordes descended. So they packed up and left for the neighboring island of Java to see if there was anything worth seeing and there, on the edge of a jungle reserve, found a flawless wave breaking near a small village called Grajagan.

They, like all surfers discovering a wave, could not believe their good fortune and stayed on the beach until their resources ran out, at which point they returned to Bali to restock. Bob drowned surfing Uluwatu days later. Bill took his brother, Mike, to Grajagan and it was Mike who had the genius idea of turning it into a surf camp where they would charge visiting surfers to stay. In making it a private, exclusive camp, they could both control the crowds and make some money.

The G-land Surf Camp opened in 1974 and a legendary cast descended upon the stilted cabins at the edge of the jungle. The people who would change surfing forever and transform it from a sideshow into the multibillion-dollar industry that Mickey Dora predicted. Into a lifestyle. Into my increasingly godforsaken career. There they were together, surfing, drugging, dreaming, but it was also at G-Land that surfing's story became completely reaffixed to cocaine's.

Mike Boyum saw potential beyond a private, exclusive surf camp. He saw oceanic trade routes that dovetailed with the desire to explore new waves and this is where the tale spins into utter mayhem with cocaine smuggling, government crackdowns, jail time, and eventual death by starvation overlooking another perfect wave in the Philippines. Or by the hands of the mafia. Or by powerful interests in Hawaii. Or by powerful interests in Australia.

His demise may be a mystery, but what came out of G-Land is not. It is the narrative through line from Peru to Hawaii to Malibu to the center console of my Volkswagen Jetta Wagon.

I thank Michael Oblowitz for his service to humanity and push out into the bright Santa Monica sun while he yells behind me to come back in and watch the Sunny Garcia film his editors are working on. I yell back that I'd rather watch his vampire porn because I don't want to watch the Sunny Garcia movie. I want to rejoice in the cinematic turn my life, and this love story, has just taken. We were smugglers. We were running away from the constraints of society, of crowds, of lame co-opters of our radical style. We needed money to find these Shambhalas, and cocaine was so easy to smuggle. Of course. It looks exactly the same as surfboard foam and is the most sensible thing in the world. I wonder if God made cocaine look like surfboard foam or was it the other way around? Did he make surfboard foam look like cocaine?

Either way, brilliant. Meant to be forever and ever and ever.

My feet float like Fred Astaire's as I dance around parking meters and bums as the stray MTV vice president of programming. A smuggler. Like Henri de Monfreid. Like the blonde Duke of Hazzard. Like a zipped-lipped lockbox of secrets and shhhhhh. But wait. I'm not a zipped-lipped lockbox of secrets. I'm a fucking surf journalist. And what is the surf journalist in this scenario? What role does he play in this grand drama?

Am I a narc?

A snitch?

I open the Volkwagen Jetta Wagon's door and collapse into the driver's seat where just weeks ago a Volcom Creedler smashed my ear to keep my mouth shut and feel all the joy drain from my heart. I am a narc. A snitch.

9

Apotheosis!

There is a fine dust floating in the air that is for sure cancerous. Generator exhaust, aerosol sunscreen, vape pen, spray paint, spray tan, spray cheese, sand particles that have been pulverized by thousands upon thousands of dirty perverted teenaged feet and sent skyward before getting sucked right into my lungs.

But I deserve it. I deserve a slow and torturous death at the hands of the surf industry since I actively work against it each and every day. Since I am a tattletale. Oh, I knew before setting out upon this hero's journey that the surf journalist was a cursed soul whose mission was to contextualize utter vapidity. But then, for one brief moment, I smelled romance, I smelled love, I smelled cocaine and thought, "Redemption!" I thought, "Make Surfing Great Again!"

But I am irredeemable. Cursed. Dying a slow cancerous irrelevant death in Huntington Beach at the US Open of Surfing trying to write a story titled "US Open: Raging rivers of urine!" Back where I began. Back where I first felt the whisper of God's voice in my surfer's ear while standing in front of the International Surfing Museum God. Surfing plus her cocaine may be the greatest love story the world has ever produced, but telling it makes me a narc and I can't be that. I can't be a fink, a canary, a stoolie, tabby, whistleblower, snitch. What would my innocent little four-year-old angel of a daughter think? She has one rule as long as she is under my wife's roof and only one: snitches get stiches. I can't set a bad example for her. I must flush my dream and accept my fate. Bottle-opener sandals and bastardized Hawaiian pidgin until I die.

And if Agenda, in Long Beach, is a tricolored mural of the five-year surf apocalypse, then the US Open of Surfing is its taste. The decayed flavor of good times turned very bad. A Mad Max-esque dystopian mess where God has officially turned his back and allows for mankind to swallow spoonful after spoonful of putrid filth.

I watch a dirty perverted teenaged boy with the words "Sexx Simbol" scrawled across his chest try and slap the ass of a dirty perverted teenaged girl with the words "Slap dat" scrawled on her lower back. Giggling from both parties ensues as he swings and misses and almost runs into a three-hundred-pound man riding a motorized chair with off-road tires featuring many Vans and Volcom stickers. A Monster Girl holding a T-shirt cannon watches too with a blank expression. I wonder if she ever fantasizes about shooting people in the face. I wonder if she could please just shoot *me* in the face. It would be a fitting end and my gravestone could read: "He died how he lived—like an asshole." Maybe I would even get a paddle out. Have you seen one of those? Where surfers paddle out on their boards together when someone dies and sit in a circle and splash water in the air and sometimes wear floral leis?

Ugh.

Much to everyone in the surf industry's chagrin, this is the biggest event of the year, and by far. Thousands upon thousands upon hundreds of thousands of perverts drain into Huntington Beach for one week near the end of July to make a mockery of decency and of my career. There are art exhibits, some skateboarding (maybe), some BMX (I think), free industry garbage like Hurley Frisbees and Mayhem temporary belly tattoos, underage drinking and a World Surf League qualifying tour event in the worst waves imaginable. There used to be live music, but it got cancelled after the 2013 US Open of Surfing turned into a riot.

That might have been one of the funnier moments in surf history. Drunk white boys with Neff bandanas tied around their faces pushing over Porta-Potties and throwing stop signs through surf shop windows to steal more Neff bandanas. Neff might be the worst brand in all of surf. On the company website, founder Shaun Neff is pictured standing like a gangster except wearing two different-colored shoes, tight black skinny jeans, some goofy Mickey Mouse T-shirt under a try-hard satin jacket, and a black beanie above the words: "We are like a gumball machine; spitting out endless flavors for the world to consume…" I wonder what "endless flavor" Huntington Beach riot tastes like. Like generator exhaust, aerosol sunscreen, vape pen, spray paint, spray tan, spray cheese, and sand particles probably.

Fucking Shaun Neff.

But who am I to judge? I make Shaun Neff look like Henri de Monfreid or the brunette Duke of Hazzard. I'm a surf journalist. A stool pigeon. The lowest of the low and depressed. Derailed. A mistake. I reach for my phone to see if surf historian Matt Warshaw has responded. I emailed him a few minutes ago wondering if the first surfer ever to get busted for cocaine was Jeff Hackman and which despised surf journalist's fault it was. He responds, "You disrespectful sloppy twink. It's HAKMAN not HACKMAN. *Surfer* published this Fred Hemmings editorial in 1969 and he points out some of the first high-profile drug users—although not by name. Scroll down to where it says 'There will be no room for dope…' and then keep reading to where Hemmings writes, 'Another once great big-wave rider's brain is like a dried prune because of dope. He now lives an unproductive existence on the slopes of Haleakala'—almost certain that's Jackie Elberle. The 'finalist in the heralded Duke contest'—I'm not sure who that is. '…the arrest of another Duke Invitational contestant on a narcotics charge one week before the contest' — that's Jeff Hakman. Fucking Hemmings, what a narco."

And for one moment I feel respite from internal torture. It wasn't a bastard surf journalist who flapped his gums about dark secrets. It was a surfer. A good, brave, historically significant one, too. Like, a proper surfer. Fred Hemmings was born in mid-1940s Hawaii to a New York father and Portuguese mother. A stud with a wide jaw and Mitt Romney / Gavin Newsom smile. He braved some of Oahu's biggest surf, won the 1968 surfing championships, later became a state senator for Hawaii, and later still a conservative talk radio host, which may explain everything.

The editorial, thankfully attached, is a bizarre work of art and I skim it on my broken phone screen while dodging underage sex crimes and unfortunate sunburns. It is titled, non-ironically, "Pro Surfing Is White" and is an unhinged screed about professionalism. "Surfing needs professionalism!" it begins and somehow goes downhill from there, making the case for some nonexistent buttoned-up class.

It's the sentence beginning "longhaired freaks and dope fiends" in which Hemmings finally gets to his point and busts out his dagger. "Although drugs seem to be in vogue with a great number of 'in' surfers today, I can assure you that there is *no* hope in dope. The pro surfers will have to be clean and healthy athletes. There will be no room for drugs. In other words, the Professional Surfing Association will help to rid our beautiful sport of the detrimental drug image."

At first I marvel at Hemmings calling out the surf world in 1969 during the Summer of Love. Him hammering the need for professionalism and drug testing right before Jimi Hendrix took the stage and jerked out the best Star Spangled Banner ever at Woodstock. But remember, again, that he was politically conservative and likely a Nixon voter. And not a surf journalist.

My shame starts to dissipate even further as I continue to move through the cancerous dust. I watch a forty-year-old wearing a Billabong x Bob Marley collaboration tank top like a mumu try to give a "free hug" to a girl drinking a sixteen-ounce can of Monster. I watch a Marine try and sneakily dump a bottle of Seagram's gin into a red plastic solo cup filled halfway with Monster and think gin and Monster is much more disgusting than Diet Coke and vodka.

And maybe I'm shallow to the point of being empty. Maybe I'm a meaningless streak across a pointless sea. Maybe I'll never carry any hashish in the hull of my ship while running from Saudis or moonshine in the trunk of my 1969 Dodge Charger while running from the

Hazzard County sheriff. Maybe everyone hates me but maybe that is the price for carrying something even better than hashish or moonshine in my heart and delivering it to the world. To pretend that surfing is a "beautiful sport" that can be teased apart from its "detrimental drug image" is to wish for surfing to be something it has never been and, if I do my surf journalist job properly, will never be. I can keep this shallow pool dirty by carrying surfing and cocaine's love story. I can keep it very unsportsmanlike. Very rude. I am not a narc.

I am a prophet.

I watch a younger kid wearing a brand-new pair of boring color-blocked Quiksilver board shorts drag a surfboard across the beach. His dad is following behind, barking surf contest strategy into his innocent ear, and I want to go up to the both and them, right then, and say, "Do you know where Quiksilver came from? Well, do you? It came from cocaine. Not figuratively, either. Literally. How's that for some contest strategy?" His dad looks like the sort that would give me a full bro lecture and I can't stomach one of those right now, so I don't— even though it is true and one of my favorite stories of all.

As the seventies swelled to a crescendo, cocaine and surfing each reached full, glorious maturity. The sixties counterculture had given way to disco fever, and cocaine, with its Dom Pérignon cache and Presidential pardon, was the go-to for a good time. The future was today and, besides a burning Middle East, nuclear saber-ratting Russians, collapsing Eastern European economies, South American wars, and unfortunate synthetic fabrics, it was time to party.

Dr. Paul Gootenberg, codirector of Latin American studies at Stony Brook University in New York, examined how cocaine changed Andean economies and pegs at least some of the spike to disco, writing, "the relationship of cocaine to 1970s disco culture cannot be stressed enough."

The drug paired delightfully with needing to be up all night while shimmying hips to the worst music ever. In New York, for example, Studio 54 was a gilded respite for disillusioned hippies. They had fought for a decade. Fought for minority rights and women's rights. Fought for ideals. Fought the police. Fought for the glories of youth and they were rewarded with Richard Nixon spying on their great hope, George McGovern. Were rewarded with a Population Bomb. And so they emptied themselves. They emptied themselves of good music, of important causes, of deeply experiential substances like LSD, and just went void. Donna Summers. And cocaine. And the artist later made famous by Billabong, Andy Warhol. And cocaine.

The legendary Casablanca Records in Los Angeles was Studio 54's West Coast equivalent. The label signed disco acts like Parliament, sure, but also broke out with glam rock sensations KISS and The Village People. Larry Harris, Casablanca's cofounder, described the scene when they went to restaurants thusly: "There was blow everywhere. It was like some sort of condiment that had to be brushed away by the waitstaff before the next party was seated. Cocaine dusted everything. It was on fingertips, tabletops, upper lips, and the floor."

David Bowie, who had moved from New York to Los Angeles, was in his Thin White Duke persona. A character that was so much better even than the blonde Duke of Hazzard. Bowie described him as "a very Aryan, fascist type; a would-be romantic with absolutely no emotion at all but who spouted a lot of neo-romance."

The Duke did not use cocaine like some sort of condiment but rather as full meal replacement. It is said that Bowie survived on a diet of cocaine, red peppers, and milk for the entire late 1970s. He described cocaine, during this period, as his "soul mate." His lover at the time, Romy Haag, said, "David didn't do lines of coke. He did bowls of it." And even though cocaine was still considered more or less benign, its downside when consumed by the bowlful, alongside milk and red peppers, manifested itself in Bowie's life as he fell into a full cocaine psychosis. He would see angels out the windows, demons coming to steal his semen, the Manson Family hiding in his closets, and piles of cocaine big as the Matterhorn—except those were real and would be consumed alongside a nice cognac.

Cocaine was everywhere. Anywhere. On everything. It had pushed through damn amphetamines, through Hitler, and come out the momentary winner. And of course the South Americans were more than happy to supply the demand. Peruvians, Colombians, Nicaraguans, and Cubans started cornering a lucrative market that was growing by tens of millions of dollars each month.

By 1979, cocaine had officially become the state of Florida's biggest import, reported to be worth over ten billion dollars a year at wholesale prices. There was fighting over the trade, sure, and many murders in Miami, and it started to sour the United States government but not really because they were also funding covert military operations with cocaine money.

Win. Win. Win. Win. Lose. Win.

Ollie North, you see, was right smack in the middle of flooding Studio 54 and Casablanca Records with cheap cocaine in order to pay for the Stinger missiles my Uncle Dave was smuggling into Afghanistan under the guise of "medical missionary." Most know about the program of selling weapons illegally to Iran in order to pay the Contras, who were fighting the commies in Nicaragua. A lesser-known component of the deal, though, was for the Contras to supplement their income by flying planes filled with cocaine up to Los Angeles and shipping it by boat to San Francisco, amping the disco fever up to eleven.

Ollie North—along with Felix Rodriguez, the Cuban American CIA operative responsible for executing Che Guevara in Bolivia—camped out in Costa Rica and packed a plane named Fat Lady with guns that would be airdropped into the Nicaraguan jungle and then sent back up to America clogged with cocaine. John Kerry, then a senator, chaired a committee looking into the Iran-Contra affair and concluded, "There is no question in my mind that people connected with the CIA were involved in drug trafficking while in support of the Contras."

There was a picture of Ollie North and my Uncle Dave on the wall of his house in Carlsbad. The two of them shaking hands in Reagan's White House. I must have stared at it for hours, studying every combed strand of Ollie North's hair. Every military medal on his chest. Every tooth in my Uncle Dave's smile. He was so proud.

I would have been, too.

They were epic pawns in an epic global smuggling game. Jeff Hakman, though, one-upped them both because he Iran Contra'd some cocaine into his fins, took it to Australia, and bought fucking Quiksilver. It is true. And he was more handsome to boot, with a jaw even twice as lantern as Fred Hemmings.

Hakman was born in the same year as Hemmings but in Redondo Beach, California, instead of Hawaii, and cool instead of lame. His dad, who worked as an aerospace engineer, bought him a gorgeous newfangled shorter surfboard when he was eight and let him cut school to surf and then moved the entire family to Oahu where Hakman really came into his own, beating Fred Hemmings as the youngest, smallest competitor at the inaugural Duke Kahanamoku Invitational held in heaving Sunset.

His newfangled shorter surfboard was all the rage, though some considered it a passing fad. Fred Hemmings, for instance, said they "are absurd for Hawaiian surf. They don't work here." But the general flow of history, thankfully, didn't agree.

The "shortboard revolution," as it later came to be called, saw surfboards drop their heights and weights in half during the late 1960s and early 1970s. It was a wild change that created super-heated infighting among the shapers of that day. On the surface, surfers may appear to be progressive and radical, but the vast majority of them are generally hamstrung by what was working yesterday. It is why the surf industry is such a total disaster. Why surf photographers whine about the Internet. Why Agenda looks like the apocalypse and the US Open of Surfing tastes like it. Why the shapers that day still don't speak to each other.

Their chopping longboards down, though, continues to reverberate. Surfing changed during the 1970s. It became angular, aggressive, jittery, radical. Turns were shortened. Nose-riding, the kind done in the water, was jettisoned because who wants to perch on the end of a longboard when you could be buried in the tube? Actually inside the ocean itself? Boards kept shrinking, kept pulling in, trying to fit in the pockets of waves seen as too critical just a few years ago. Trying to disco on the water with disco-sized crowds. These were the boards that the G-Land explorers took with them as they escaped. And this is the board that Jeff Hakman glassed cocaine in before traveling to Australia.

His plan was simple. Cocaine was cheap in the United States, thanks to Ollie and my Uncle Dave, but it was expensive in Australia. Heroin, on the other hand, was cheap in Australia but expensive in the United States. Hakman did the rudimentary math and decided to benefit from this economic peculiarity.

And so he took off with his cocaine surfboard, and won the 1976 Bells Beach surf event while totally loaded, and I'm sure he would have just come home with a new heroin surfboard except he saw a pair of Quiksilver trunks on a fellow competitor and knew that a surf trunk that fits properly is better than heroin, though probably not as good as cocaine.

Hakman negotiated the rights to the US license, as legend has it, by drunkenly eating a doily in front of Quiksilver's Australian creator, paid for it with his cocaine money, and the rest is history. Quiksilver trunks, sleek, short, durable, bright, were exactly what the kids wanted. And overnight the surf industry was born.

There is something about it that makes sense today—that the kids would be drawn toward a tanned, pointless rebellion. A totally un-dogmatic reimagining of what mattered in the world and that the kids would buy the clothes that represented it. At the time, though, I think it was only confusing to the surfers leading this bold revolution. Surfing is an insular thing. Surfers' minds are rotted equally by salt and cocaine and we are only ever confused. The men who started Quiksilver—and just on its heels Rip Curl, Billabong, O'Neill, Body Glove, Rusty, etc.—worked in their garages to make things they needed and their friends needed.

Trunks that wouldn't rip.

Wetsuits to keep warm.

Surfboards.

It was never supposed to become a thing. It was never supposed to catch on.

But it did catch and it caught enough to reverberate across the sands of Huntington Beach today, even though it is a total bastardization of the pointless rebellion. Even though right now I am watching a gym-fit fifty-year-old with shaved arms and True Religion jeans flex and preen in a Rip Curl "Live The Search" T-shirt. I am watching a spray-tanned mom in Quiksilver's Roxy give her twelve-year-old daughter a sixteen-ounce Monster.

Bizarre, really, and all thanks to cocaine. All thanks to Jeff Hakman and his mini-Iran-Contra. Oh, of course the amount of cocaine being consumed by the infant surf industry didn't match the concurrent disco-glam late-1970s club scene, but nothing did. And again, music, restauranteering, art, finance, politics, and sport are all fickle. Cocaine today, heroin tomorrow, adaptocrine the day after that. Cocaine and surfing were born together, grew together. Cocaine gave life to the surf industry and then it was surfing's turn to set cocaine off.

I am watching three clean-cut USC frat boys prancing about in fluorescent sunglasses with various suggestive phrases written on their shaved chests. I am watching a pack of giggling preteen girls dressed in throwback eighties neon from Hollister with messages that read GIRLS JUST WANNA HAVE SUN and SAVE A WAVE, RIDE A SURFER. I'm watching a Newport Beach mom flap out a beach towel that says RAD! in bold angular font and wonder if any of them know about the love note they're all retroactively broadcasting.

And it hits me like a kilo brick. Now I know exactly the path my journey must take. The internal defeat at being a narc has evaporated completely. I really *am* a prophet.

The sun has begun its descent, throwing longer shadows over the debauchery, and I haven't felt this driven since wanting to be a fake medical missionary. Or since at least last week. I must finish my trek up the mountain, like Moses, and bring down the love story that makes David Bowie look like a fickle spouse. That makes Keith Richards look like a sensible but wishy-washy lightweight.

It is time to go to Laguna Beach.

10

The Ultimate Boon!

Laguna Beach at sunset is unparalleled in its beauty. Oh, sure, the MTV show *Laguna Beach: The Real Orange County* did its best to destroy any vestige of beauty hidden in the sleepy Orange County cockles, and maybe the Fox show *The O.C.* did it worse even though that one mostly pilloried Newport Beach instead of Laguna. Do you remember those? Lauren Conrad and Mischa Barton? Son of a bitch, but still. When the sun starts its slide down the sky and lights the hills and lights the air and lights the spirit, it is the most beautiful place on earth.

I pause, check my phone, then stare at the ocean for a minute watching the sun dancing on the waves, turning red, orange, yellow. The warm breeze smells like jasmine, coconut oil, and surf wax. A pelican glides low, almost touching the water with its magnificent wings. New Audis drive both north and south on the Pacific Coast Highway. It is a strange thing about Orange County, a geographical oddity. Billionaires who live here drive new Audis. A6s, A8s, Q7s. The poorest who live here drive new Audis. A4s, A6s, Q7s. A very strange thing. Orange County has flattened wealth, drained all nuance from class stratification. Some of the richest people in the United States dwell behind the Orange Curtain and it is impossible to tell them apart from some of the most middle-class people in the United States and even some people who are properly poor, or as poor as someone can be in Orange County. It might sound nice, like an egalitarian paradise, but have you ever been? There is something very off about it. Very wrong. And if you don't believe me, watch reruns of *Laguna Beach*. Watch Lauren Conrad and her friends live completely monotone, without any nuance or even so much as a hint of it.

I'm thinking about Lauren Conrad and her friends while watching the sun sink farther and farther, but also thinking about cocaine and checking my phone, again, when the heckling starts. "Hey, bro. You gonna go shred? Sick. I bet you shred sick." I turn around ready to get angry but see a pack of the raddest ten-year-olds on earth hanging over a rail, looking at me. Blonde hair hanging over eyes. Each one blonder than the last, severely tanned heads with razor- sharp neck tan lines even though it is summer. Brand-new sparkling white Former T-shirts. One is wearing a beanie at peak jaunty. The surfed-out Orange County preteen sits at the very top of any social pecking order, so flawless in game that even Ragnar Lodbrok would wilt beneath the laser of his attention.

I panic and run into the nearby Laguna Surf and Sport without thinking. To a place even more pressure-filled than the mean streets, or at least a place that used to be. The California surf shop was once a bastion of all things cool. The boards, the trunks, the clothes, board bags, magazines, VHS surf videos, Lagwagon soundtrack, and especially the shop workers. Grown-up surfed-out Orange County preteens who would mock hapless customers from behind glass counters filled with surf stickers.

I remember stepping through the doors and into the fog of sweet surf wax as an Oregonian youth on family trips down south. I would gaze lovingly, longingly at the merchandise that I couldn't afford. I would run my hand along the rails of boards I could only dream of owning. Sometimes a shop worker would ask if I needed any help in the most laconic way possible, usually while flipping through a surf magazine and not looking up to make eye contact. My heart would seize and I would mutter something and flee, trying not to gaze at the Sex Wax in the glass counter, lest anyone catch me and think I was a blushing debauchee.

The shop worker in Laguna Surf and Sport asks me if he can help me find anything. He is standard surf cool and I feel the muscle memory of a kooky youth but swallow hard and make a panic impulse buy instead of running away. A red-and-black Laguna Surf and Sport trucker hat. He seems appreciative and probably is. The surf shop has fallen on hard times, even harder than the rest of American retail. Online shopping, changing habits, fast fashion, etc., have all cut into already slim margins, plus the surf shop is tasked with selling the apocalypse. The Volcoms, Reefs, Quiksilvers, and Billabongs that nobody wants to buy anymore.

The hat definitely won't fit my skinny head but I feel happy giving a small drop of life support to my childhood nirvana and head back out into the perfect evening, check my phone, and try to find a place to kill some time where the raddest ten-year-olds on earth don't lurk.

A neon light across the street advertises sushi.

Laguna somehow has more great Japanese-owned, Japanese-staffed, Japanese-chefed sushi restaurants anywhere I have been outside of Japan. Their menus feature fantastic mash-ups like teriyaki chicken versions of spicy buffalo wings and pasta made out of shitake mushrooms. I trust my nemeses don't have fully developed palates yet and so I head over, push through the door, and am promptly seated by a smiling woman from Chigasaki. I watch the orange sunshine finish its dip into the ocean.

Before Lauren Conrad and the Audis, this place might have been most famous for Orange Sunshine, the acid made and distributed by The Brotherhood of Eternal Love. The 1970s gang, made up mostly of surfers, based itself in a Laguna Beach head shop named Mystic Arts World and hoped to start a psychedelic revolution in the United States by producing and distributing their delicious Orange Sunshine acid. Mike Hynson, from *Endless Summer* fame, was part of the group, as was David Nuuhiwa, one of the best nose-riders ever and son of a legendary Waikiki beach boy. The feds raided Laguna Beach in 1972 and sent the Brotherhood around the world. Mostly to places with good waves.

But I'm not here for acid. I am here for cocaine. To find the love story that makes Robert Downey Jr. look like a quitter. To find Michael

Tomson, one of the greatest characters surfing has ever produced. He is my synthesis. He is the death of conservatism. He is exactly what I need.

I texted him from the sands of Huntington, telling him I was coming, but was too excited so raced my Volkswagen Jetta Wagon south before receiving a response. Past Newport, Corona Del Mar, past Crystal Cove. Past Audi A6, Audi A8, Audi Q7, and even the odd Audi TT before stopping in his hometown of Laguna. I check my phone for the hundredth time and still nothing.

A lady with injected lips has just come in and is trying to tell the Japanese sushi chef that her Shi-Tzu is a service dog. "But he totally is," she whines in perfect Real Housewife intonation. "She provides so many services to me all the time."

The sushi chef is not having it and bows, slightly, while repeating, "Sorry. Sorry. Sorry…" with a pained smile pulled across his face.

Quintessentially Japanese.

And maybe Michael Tomson has something do with the magic Japan-Laguna connection because he, quite basically, made Comme de Garçons into a surf brand. He traveled across the Pacific with a head full of inspiration, invented surf fashion and what it really meant to look and act like a surfer. Forever changing my life in the process.

As the 1970s transitioned to the 1980s, surfing transitioned, too. The surf industry was young but vibrant, the beaches were crowded and a new, and violent localism was rearing its head, or at least it was according to the mainstream media. Surfers have always been territorial. Hawaiian kings crushing bones, sneaking their waves, Mickey Dora and Tubesteak slapping ho-dads in Malibu, rock-throwing in Palos Verdes, but early 1980s stories in *Newsweek* and *Esquire* took it all a few steps further and detailed how "surf gangs" went around with guns and knives, menacing outsiders and fighting rival surf gangs. I wish this were true because *Mad Max Beach* is more interesting than the professional turn that was actually happening.

Surf contests, like localism, had been around since almost the beginning. I don't know if the Peruvian fishermen judged each other for their performances, but the ancient Hawaiians did, and most beaches would have small contests to decide which surfer was best. A few big-prize-money contests took place around the world, too, but there was no judging uniformity or champion crowned across multiple events.

Fred Hemmings, in his desire to drive dope from surfing and make it professional and Republican, first made a list simply by ranking the surfers who went to the bigger contests by how much prize money they made that year. The International Professional Surfers tour was born in 1975 and surfing started to become an actual profession.

The IPS grew in fits and starts and only had limited success in reaching a broader audience, so in 1982, Australian Ian Cairns, who once performed in a surfing boy band called The Bronzed Aussies, revolted and formed the Association of Surfing Professionals. With money from Op, a former surf brand giant, he peeled most of the surfers over, expanded the number of contests per year, and kicked the total purse up by a few hundred thousand dollars—and he made Hemmings cry.

One of the most exciting surfers on the new ASP tour was a debonair South African by the name of Shaun Tomson. He was every mother's dream. Tall, thin, tan, nice jaw, soft-spoken, talented, a one-time Calvin Klein model. A Jewish gentleman with classic athlete faux humility. Surf journalist Phil Jarratt wrote, "In an era filled with rough-hewn Australians and streetwise Hawaiians, Tomson strode in like the Great Gatsby."

Shaun won the 1977 ISP Championship and stayed near the top as the ISP became the ASP. He changed how people ride barrels, how they compete, how they surf in general, but it is his cousin that I am waiting on right now because, though Michael never touched real competitive success, he was the actual Great Gatsby. He was the one who made surfing into a flameout party.

And I'm about ready to abandon restraint and give him a call when a conversation on the other side of a shoji screen distracts me. "Yeah, I totally got tendinitis in my shoulder from towing Taj out in the surf of bigger days. I haven't MRI'd it yet but I have an appointment next week. Been super lame on my surfing."

I stand up and peek over. Two forty-five-year-old realtors sit across the table from each other eating truffle edamame with forks. One is wearing a skintight dark blue polo shirt. The other is wearing a skintight dark grey polo shirt. Both have salt-and-pepper hair.

"I surfed Lowers with him today, though. We walked down and he totally killed it," Dark Blue continues.

"Sick," Dark Grey responds.

"Yeah. We did, like, a little soul surfing thing just to break it up a little. It was so rad. What about your groms? How old are they?"

"Bro, they're, like, ten, five, and one," Dark Grey says between bites. "I've got the ten-year-old in a junior surf training program coming up this summer. He's such a little pro already. Like fully knows how to surf with tactics. I saw him paddle-battling his friend the other day, trying to get priority. So rad. I'm going to take him to the US Open tomorrow and have him watch the Pro Junior heats so he can really learn how to maximize the wave's scoring potential. You know, getting that little bash on the inside section. The one-year-old will probably need some work. He doesn't seem too competitive."

"Sick…" Dark Blue nods. "That's killer. Hey, you should go down to Mexico. It was decent last month, a little fat but still rad, and such a good place to work on tactics. Some of the local guys were hyped but fully suck and you can totally burn them. We were just down for a couple days and fully brought the kids. Have you done it? Have you brought the kids? There's not a lot of pressure out there. So chill. The locals can't surf. You want your kids to have confidence. Building the foundation for that one key activity…"

I sit back down, angry that this is what surfing has become. Angry that realtors are attempting to raise professional surfers while eating edamame with forks. Angry that there is any such thing as a surf training program. Knowing that this is why the surf industry is in a five-year apocalypse. Sure, the raddest ten-year-olds on earth still surf, but how much longer will it be considered cool with skintight polos turning it into a sport? With the damned conservative mission creep. And this is why I need Michael Tomson. I reach for my phone and still nothing, so I spend eight minutes writing "Huntington Beach: Riot City, USA!" on BeachGrit where I propose throwing a BeachGrit-sponsored riot at next year's US Open of Surfing. That'll teach the realtors. Surfing is for derelicts, not little tacticians.

And somehow it's as if my story nudges God because the moment I post it, my phone rings. Could it be? Might it be?

It is. Michael Tomson. Like he was listening from his manor on the hill, waiting to rescue me from this bastardization. God bless the man. I tell him I'm coming over.

He barks, "Come! But where are you?" in his perfect South African inflected English. I tell him Laguna.

"Oh..." he responds. "I don't live in Laguna anymore. I've moved to San Clemente. I'll send you my address. COME!" The way he barks "come" again sounds very Al Pacino in *Heat*.

I pay as quickly as I can and scamper outside, away from the grom talk and surf training. The lady with injected lips is sitting at a table by the door complaining to the waitress about the wind and telling her Shi-Tzu that she doesn't get any sushi today. I tell her she should feed him cocaine and feel untouchable, like one of the raddest ten-year-olds on earth. Smart and sassy.

11

Refusal of the Return!

I find my Volkswagen Jetta Wagon and punch it through Laguna while a Sam Smith cover of Whitney Houston's 1985 classic "How Will I Know?" plays on repeat. It is all slow and whiney and piano-y. Not eighties electric drums and keytar kinetic. Why would Sam Smith do that? Why would he take the fun out? Why would he rob Whitney Houston's pep? Her version sounded like cocaine. Sam Smith's sounds like prescription pill abuse.

It really is a wonder that cocaine transitioned from the disco dance floor to the go-go eighties without losing any steam. Gaining steam, even. Becoming a necessary component of yuppie life alongside skinny piano ties and giant mobile phones. It somehow didn't retain any disco taint—the wacky hair and glittery pantsuits, the Earth, Wind & Fire— even though it was so closely associated with the era.

Maybe it was because Ollie North had flooded the market, making it cheaper and more accessible than ever and further farm crises in South America kept coca as the most lucrative crop. Maybe because yuppies needed to wake up earlier to make all that fast money and go to bed later, after 11:00 p.m. reservations at Dorsia. Maybe because cocaine paired with rayon even better than it did with polyester. Whatever the case, by the mid-1980s the cocaine market was absolutely saturated.

It was a time of greed, Gordon Gecko, and Gotcha—Michael Tomson's surf fashion label that turned the industry into an actual force.

Michael had been born in Durban, South Africa, to European parents and had surfed in professional contests during the early 1970s in South Africa, Australia, and most notably Hawaii, where he was part of a brash pack that changed the approach to the world's most famous wave. He was fearless at the Banzai Pipeline. Aggressive, raw, and powerful in his approach. Up to that time, Pipe was considered a goofy foot's domain since they rode facing the wave. Michael, and a motley crew of Australians and his cousin Shaun, showed that it could be ridden just as gorgeously backside as frontside.

Professional surfing couldn't hold all of his attention, though, and toward the late 1970s he became a full-fledged surf journalist alongside sometime competitor, starting his own magazine in Durban and becoming an assistant editor at *Surfing* in America. The same *Surfing* where I was once a retained writer and editor-at-living-large. The same *Surfing* that is now dead.

Michael knew, always knew, that surfing wasn't for everyone and couldn't be marketed to the masses—or at least not as a sport. He wrote, "Potential surf fans in Ohio and Michigan want a blood-busting winner, one they can understand because they can see the bastard who gets from A to B first…" smelling Dark Blue Polo and Dark Blue Button-Down from four decades away. He knew that professionalism was death. That forming surfing in the shape of Ohio and Michigan was the end.

And I wonder why Michael Tomson moved to San Clemente himself as I drive past Salt Creek, past Dana Point, past Capistrano Beach. Past Audi A4, Audi A8, Audi Q3, and even the odd Audi Allroad. He was Laguna Beach. He defined the city as much as the Brotherhood of Eternal Love. More than the Pageant of the Masters, Laguna's sad art festival where people are dressed as classical works of art and stand around like dimwits while even bigger dimwits "ooh" and "aah" at the misbegotten majesty.

He told me the story once before. "Here's how I ended up in Laguna. I was living in San Clemente. Bob McKnight, from Quiksilver, was pissed off at me because I was starting Gotcha. San Clemente was too far south, so I said to my friend, 'Let's just drive up and see what there is.' Driving through Laguna, I looked up and thought, 'This place looks cool.' So we pull over. That afternoon we were in a house and that's where we actually formed the company. That's how it happened. Through the course of time, Laguna became THE surf town. Really. And it is. It's the center of the industry."

That was in 1979, and Gotcha set off like a rocket. I remember seeing it in the surf shops where I loitered as a petrified Oregonian youth. The fluorescents, the cuts, the boldness, the half fish/half man logo. It was all so cool, so impossibly cool, and I knew I didn't belong so I would buy cheap knockoff brands like Pirate Surf and past-their-prime Op and Maui & Sons instead. My cousins, Uncle Dave's kids, wore Gotcha and sassed their parents. I remember seeing the Gotcha ads in the few surf magazines I would buy: Full double-page ads featuring some kook on the first page in black and white. A bald old man holding a brown paper sack. A skinny kid with a tucked-in T-shirt and an egg-shaped head. Two very fat kids wearing tank tops. The words IF YOU DON'T SURF, DON'T START printed beneath their sad frames. The second page featuring some amazing Gotcha team rider, always fit, always tan, always totally ripping. He's got the words IF YOU SURF, NEVER STOP.

My mom always thought the ads were mean-spirited. She thought the surf magazines were morally bankrupt in general, with their objectification of women and glorification of a viscerally shallow pursuit, but it was Gotcha's sneering "get lost" that got her the worst. She would get angry at me for pinning them on my bedroom walls, and she was right. They were mean-spirited but that is what made Gotcha the dream. It was exclusive, and you weren't invited, and I wasn't invited, but son of a bitch I wanted to be as I lounged in my tiny Coos Bay bedroom. I wanted to be more than anything in the entire world and even thought about sassing my mom and telling her to get lost. It was what surfing always should have been. A repudiation of big-tent growth, of professionalism, of conservatism. A celebration of the tiny few.

I wind up into San Clemente's hills, past Molly Bloom's Irish Bar where *Surfing Magazine* was put into the ground, past a telephone banner praising the local surfing Gudauskas brothers, past professional surfer super-prodigy turned vague disappointment Kolohe Andino's last-century mid-modern, around the bend, and park in front of the address Michael had given me. The house is nice but nondescript. Like everything else in Orange County. I ring the doorbell and wonder if he had to move because of cocaine.

During Gotcha's run, Michael Tomson was a notorious party monster, with cocaine being his belle. After Gotcha's run, when he became president of the Surf Industry Manufacturing Association, he was a notorious party monster, with cocaine being his dame. Five years ago, he was a notorious party monster, getting busted by the cops with $2,000 of blow in his pocket. His sweetie. Just last year, he was a notorious party monster, getting busted by the cops in his Laguna home with so much cocaine that they slapped him with an "intent to distribute" charge. *The Los Angeles Times* put it thusly: "Former professional surfer and cofounder of the Gotcha surfwear company was arrested on suspicion of felony drug trafficking, Laguna Beach police said. On June 18 officers conducted a probation check of Michael Elliot Tomson's house on Mar Vista Avenue and found 'items consistent with selling narcotics and fifty-two grams of cocaine,' Sgt. Tim Kleiser wrote in an email."

His gal. His one and only. And that is a four-decade run. A forty-year dance. Never turning his head. Never taking another out on the floor. David Bowie left cocaine behind in the mid-1980s, saying, "I've an addictive personality, and it took hold of my life. I'm ambivalent about it now. It was an extraordinary thing to have to go through. I wouldn't want to go through it again, but I'm sort of glad I did." And is there anything more painful than watching a love grow cold? Than watching one lover become ambivalent about the other?

Keith Richards had many partners but left cocaine behind over a decade ago when, according to his biography, he fell from a tree while foraging for coconuts after a few bumps and split his head open. Even at the height of his romance, though, he seems too in control to be truly in love, writing, "I was very meticulous about how much I took. I'd never put more in to get a little higher. It's the greed involved that never really affected me. People think once they've got this high, if they take some more they're going to get a little higher. There's no such thing. Especially with cocaine."

And that may be sensible but it ain't passion. It ain't out of control. It ain't burn the stage down. It ain't Shakespearean. And Shakespearean is what is going to save surf.

Michael Tomson is Shakespearean.

He was always unapologetic. He always seemed like if people cared about his lifestyle, then that was their problem, not his. The surf industry, for its part, has always been embarrassed, ready to brush Tomson and Gotcha under the nearest carpet. The surf media somewhere between uninterested and paternalistic. Phil Jarratt, legendary Australian surf journalist, wrote after Tomson's latest arrest, "I loved to watch Michael surf, but our friendship was built on our shared love of good writing, magazine design concepts and, it has to be said, the devil's dandruff. This was the seventies and coke was unavoidable, but some people constructed better avoidance plans than we did. There were plenty of all-nighters, washing the stuff down with whiskey and wine, arguing with increasingly scary intensity the relative merits of Tom Wolfe and Hunter S. Thompson. I look back on those times with more pleasure than regret, but we all knew it was a phase we were going through. Or most of us did. In the eighties, I dropped back into mainstream journalism and he went into business, and I didn't see much of Michael for a few years. When we reconnected, Gotcha had made him a millionaire but already he'd put much of the profits up his nose. His coke bingeing was an open secret in the surf industry and he was already on the police watch list. Pulled over for speeding one night on the 405, he threw a vial of coke under the wheels of the thundering freeway traffic before the cops frisked him. They looked him up and down, thinking, only a matter of time."

Again, the growing-out-of-a-phase, the restraint, the let's-all-grow-up-and-be-adults is not the stuff of legend. It is the stuff of half measures. Of not falling head over heels. Of hedging. What if Romeo had kept Rosaline on the hook in case Juliet didn't work out? What if he was sensible? Maybe he would have lived, sure, but what kind of life? Not a glorious romantic one, for damn sure.

The door flies open and my Romeo is standing there, hair still perfectly frosted and reaching toward the sky, black sweats, black T-shirt. He is still an imposing figure and his South African bark reaches through the still warm night and embraces me. "Chas! Welcome. Can you believe this shit? I live in San Clemente now. Come in."

I follow him through his entryway, down a small flight of stairs and to the living room. It is not decorated like his old Laguna house which featured memories of a life well lived. Gorgeous surf shots of Michael laid back in a gaping Pipeline tube. Coffee table books about Gotcha. It is clean but normal. An overstuffed couch. A coffee table with no books.

I take the couch, he falls into an overstuffed chair and says, "I keep thinking of you. You were telling me before about a pirate boat somewhere. What were you doing there?" The last time I had been with Michael was right before going to Djibouti. I'm surprised he still remembers and tell him about the ketch, Red Sea, Saudi Arabia, terrorism, antiterrorism legislation, a raging civil war, and a four-foot pirate named Mosquito. I tell him the goal was to actually live bigger than life for a moment, to cast off what I felt were shackles and do something romantic.

He takes it in for a minute and rubs his chin. Staring a hole through me before leaning forward and asking, "Why don't you write fiction?"

I laugh.

"I can't. My crusted brain can't conceive of characters richer or better than ones who exist in real life, like Eddie Rothman. Frankly, I don't think anyone could. He is impossible to conjure."

He leans forward and points a tanned finger at me.

"Characters. You've got to have characters. Elmore Leonard kind of characters. Whenever I'm reading these things, one of his books, and I've read them all twice, some three times, I think, 'This guy creates characters that *do* something…'"

—and he barks the word *do*—

"The what for is in the characters. The story is in the characters. And they are so *fucking* hip…"

—and he barks the word *fucking*—

"…so *fucking* good it is actually unbelievable. I'll put a Leonard book down when I'm done with it and think, what was that about? But it was just entertaining. Did you read Leonard's *Djibouti* when you were in Djibouti?"

I tell him that I read it as soon as I got home and it was truly amazing. Djibouti is a difficult-to-navigate hell pit. A pirate town but not necessarily in a sexy way. A mad geopolitical ragout where Russia, Germany, the United States, Japan, and France each have large military forces running live weapons drills and carrying out top-secret missions within spitting distance of each other. After hours, those who can get day passes mingle in the decrepit, portico'd town center drinking Heineken in shabby joints, where Ethiopian girls shimmy and pimps offer their services for a night, glaring at each other while melting in oven-like heat. And somehow, even though he had never been, Elmore captured its essence, writing better than I ever could, writing, "The place is the gateway to Islam. Or the back door to the West, the dividing line between God and Allah."

Oh, that's just so damned good, and I tell Michael how delicious Leonard's description of Djibouti was. He grins a mischievous grin and nods while saying, "It's all about the characters. He has this dialogue, man. His dialogue was so *fucking* taut, so *fucking*—"

"I can't do dialogue. I can't create characters…" I cut in. "You exist and you are better than I could create."

He stops, sits back, and chuckles, "Oh, I'm your guy then."

And I don't explain, I don't mumble some preface. I just ask, "So where the fuck did we go wrong?"

He doesn't need an explanation. He doesn't need a preface. He doesn't even need clarification as to who "we" are. He knows.

"I'll tell you. We fucking drank our own Kool-Aid. That's what it came down to. I can't tell you in two thousand when, see, you've got to understand the footprint right. So it starts off with just little surf shops then Gotcha comes along and we're selling sportswear. Surf fashion. That is the key thing. Surf as a fashion statement. I get nominated for best West Coast men's designer TWICE in eighty-five and eighty-seven. Milan, Tokyo, New York, Paris. Runways are having surf looks. It has become the thing. Surf goes from this coastal beach thing in California, Hawaii, Florida, to suddenly Seventh Avenue. You know what I mean? It explodes. Right behind that comes the footprint. PacSun. Prior to PacSun the surf industry was small. PacSun brought five hundred doors. Later on Zumiez, but PacSun brought five hundred doors right away. They exploded the footprint. Then, thereafter, it was almost like action sports followed that. Surf became board sports. We kind of tried with snowboarding stuff and...nobody has ever cracked the skate world. In history. They are a group of people that refuse to be targeted. And they are the perfect underlying fucking customer. So board sports became Fuel TV and all that. Do you remember that? All that fucking shit. And then suddenly, in combination with fashion going away from surf, from board sports, to the Internet, the whole thing fucking imploded. The big shakedown happened from two thousand eight."

PacSun, or Pacific Sunwear of California, began as a small 1980s surf shop in Newport Beach but soon saw the potential of the exploding interest in surf culture and moved into malls across America. Bringing the dream, almost overnight, directly to the Midwest, Northeast, Southeast, and Southwest. Places without surf but with a hunger for the fashion. And this was the beginning of the surf industry apocalypse. The slide to oblivion. The Mick Fanning beer-bottle sandals. The brands' coffers swelled, but all of a sudden there was a new consumer and this consumer didn't surf.

Thankfully Gotcha died years before this happened, burning up in a big ball of neon fire, growing too big, going too wild, and finally selling to Perry Ellis in the mid-1990s. It changed hands a few times after that but has never come back, with Tomson saying, "My baby turned into a fucking whore."

But the baby was a mean-spirited little bitch before she was a fucking whore. The baby made my mom question the morality of surf culture and whipped kids into a frenzy. The surf shops couldn't keep Gotcha in stock and not just because they were selling it. Little surf rats with no money but lots of bravado would brazenly steal it off the racks. The less brave would steal the fish-man hangtag. It was rebellious, punk, the in crowd that ruthlessly made fun of the out crowd. And I ask Michael why he exacerbated potential customers. Why did he tell people who didn't surf not to start?

He looks at me like it is the most sensible thing in the world, smashing a tanned fist into his hand while starting to growl, starting to find a kinetic rhythm.

"That really was at the heart of the matter because surf was so crowded. Longboards had happened. Prior to that there were no longboards, man. Longboards were historical but they weren't a lifestyle. And in the early nineties they became a lifestyle. Actually the late eighties. Everyone was riding a fucking longboard. At Lowers! You know what I mean? I couldn't even surf Lowers anymore. Idiots were dropping in, you know. So that longboard thing happened and brought in all fucking new customers. Boys, girls, kids, old people, suddenly…you know, the nucleus of surf was being polluted. That's where 'if you don't surf, don't start' came from. And it resonated, you know. People dug it."

Lowers, or Lower Trestles, in San Clemente, is California's most recognized high-performance wave breaking almost year 'round over rugged cobblestones. The way it pitches and runs is perfect for airs, for progression, and that is exactly what surfing is. Progression. Or at least what it should be. It wasn't for people looking for a chill time. It wasn't for sportsmen. It wasn't for historical buffs. It wasn't for mellow-soul types. It wasn't for people who wanted to feel the glide, flow, energy, rhythm of the universe. Surfing belonged to the radical few and Michael was determined to drive a wedge between the in and the out with his brand. The surfers who rode for Gotcha carried this devil-may-care ethos. The advertisements pushed it. And the parties celebrated it.

Brand managers, team managers, executive vice presidents, surf journalists, and professional surfers still whisper about Gotcha's parties even though the last one happened twenty-odd years ago. Some whisper in tones of hushed reverence. Some with underlying notes of negative moralizing. But all whisper. And I tell him, "Gotcha's parties are legendary. I still hear people talking about them. People who weren't even there. I was never there, but I dream. And people always talk about the sheer amount of cocaine."

He sits back in his chair and groans. It is, at once, the sound of appreciation for a vast monument but also the exhausting toll. I continue.

"Nobody throws parties like that anymore. I mean, every surf party has cocaine, maybe even as much as ever, but it is always so hidden. So wrapped up. And the parties don't feel unhinged. They feel tired. Why?"

"I don't know," he says, leaning back into his overstuffing, looking deflated for the first time. "Nobody else cares about cocaine. Music, fashion, they don't give a fuck. In surf it's a fucking big no-no even though more people here do coke than in any other industry. I can tell you right now, there aren't too many people in positions of power that don't do it."

"But why?" I ask, wanting more. Wanting to find the thing, the promise, to bring down the mountain back to the surf industry. Wanting to figure out where the disconnect is. Wanting to break the whole thing open.

Michael leans forward again, filling with life, breathing deeper and I can hear a whistling in his nose where a septum once was.

"You are absolutely right. Those fucking parties. Well, they were fashion shows that became parties. We used to do things," he starts before correcting himself. "Well, *I* used to do things like James Brown impersonators, naked chicks—fully naked—walking down these aisles and dancing. Not a stitch of clothing on and spray-painted in neon colors. It was fucking unreal. It was OUTRAGEOUS."

And he shouts the word "outrageous," letting it bounce off the mostly empty walls of his new San Clemente home.

"What I did was that I didn't really care. At that point in time there wasn't any history to follow so we were just doing it. I made fucking pants that were short. It was, show me something fucking new or get the fuck out of the office. You know what I mean? And the parties followed the same format. Everything was new. Everything was big. Everything was fresh. It felt like surfing for the first time."

And I'm curious suddenly about why he quit surfing on the tour. It would have been a dream, I'd imagine, in those early days. Traveling the world without a care, experiencing new places, new waves, competing, smashing opponents, and suddenly I wonder if maybe he is not a competitive person? If being the best doesn't drive him, so I ask.

He pauses, really pondering his internal makeup. "That's a good question. I was and I wasn't. In my mind, I could never only focus on surf. You know what I mean? I was eclectic. Which is where a lot of the fruits of my life came from anyway. But there is a certain monosyllabic monotony to winning in a sport. You have to be dedicated and alone in that. You can't let anything else distract you, you know what I mean? It's kind of a weird space. I always just had ulterior interests. I'm competitive at wanting to be the best at something. I'm not so competitive at a one-on-one deal. Surfing, not these days for sure, but at the time. At Pipe. I was competitive. For sure. No question. I was there. Nobody backs out."

Surfing, real surfing, and any conversation about real surfing, always inevitably comes back to Pipeline on Oahu's North Shore. It is the wave that both defines and creates the brightest stars. No surf legend has ever walked without placing his marker on Pipeline. I ask if he still surfs Pipe and he almost jumps out of his chair, screaming, "Never! Wouldn't even CONSIDER it. It is terrifying, man! There comes a point in time when it doesn't matter how hard you've trained, how fit you are, how many hours you've put in, how good your equipment is. Fuck all. You're still not going to make that drop and it's because of reflex. You don't have that reflex. At the time you're not thinking. But thinking can get you caught from behind which is…like right now. I would never consider riding a wave like that and once you start to question it then it's over."

Which makes me wonder if there are parallels with business and parallels with cocaine. Is there a time to quit? Were David Bowie and Keith Richards right? I ask if he feels he could start another brand today, one that would bring the violent fun back to surfing, that would crush the conservative monster, or if it feels the same as paddling out at Pipeline without the same reflexes.

"I couldn't do it and I'll tell you what. It's not necessarily from not having the talent. I'll tell you the difference: technology. The whole way you market products today. I knew before, I could envisage the future. *Clearly*. That was in nineteen eighty-five. I could not do that today. The Internet, the way consumers use digital. I didn't grow up digital. It's a fucking big difference, man. It's not natural, you know what I'm saying? I can hire people to do that, but it isn't me. And I go through the motions and all this. I do all the fucking things I'm supposed to do but I don't intuit that way, and that's a huge difference. You get older and your role becomes different." He gets up, slowly, and says, "Let's go drink some wine."

I follow him to the kitchen rolling over what he's said in my head. About change and technology and movement. Watching him move. There are the hints of the way he used to surf Pipeline, aggressive, raw, and powerful, but also stiff. It's lifestyle that has clearly taken a physical toll. The cocaine. The Matterhorns of cocaine.

He pours me an almost-too-good-to-be-true glass of Sancerre then pours himself one. Crisp, clean. Bracing acidity. Flinty smoke flavors. We both lean on the kitchen island looking at each other. I take a sip, savor, and ask, "Is cocaine a creative drug for you?"

He takes a sip and thinks for a minute.

"You know something, I couldn't articulate that. Irony is my real form of creativity. You know, I don't say I'm going to drink to do this or do the drug to do that. It's just a lifestyle. To me it's about…where I get good is when I get my engine going, I turn on all the inputs and I look at different stuff and I start musing and wondering about things. Points of reference, whether they be magazines or online or books or ways of saying things or images I see. I am a huge collector of stuff. An importer, that's what I am. The edge that Gotcha had over everyone was my nationality. I came from a European background and I was all over the world all the time importing stuff. Not products. *Ideas*. Whereas everyone here was designing in this little enclave of Orange County, I was in the fucking world.

"I was such a furious shopper. I would go down the street in Tokyo, in Paris, in London. I'd walk in, give the guy a credit card, and say hang on to it. Then I'd come back and collect my purchases. I would buy ten-K of clothing in one day. The shit I have here right now. Two storage facilities. So much Comme de Garçons, Yohji Yamamoto. So much stuff it is frightening. I was out with players, man. Johnny Rotten is like my brother. I made his clothes and could tell you some fucking stories that could make your hair stand on end."

"Tell me…" I say as much voyeuristically as journalistically.

He sighs then laughs. "I can't say these things. The drug stories. I was doing some really strange things, let's just put it that way. I once went, for example, to a meeting in Europe and I left the shit at home. So I just went back to the airport and flew home, got it and flew back. But I never wanted to expose anyone so I never told anyone where I went so nobody even ever knew. Thirty-six hours."

Michael's not wanting to expose others to his demons is something he has mentioned to me before. There is a sort of chivalry to his dance with cocaine. He was generous with it but didn't want his own slide deeper, deeper, deeper to derail the general good time. From every account, Gotcha's aesthetic mirrored the tension between a good time and an over-the-cliff disaster. It was always teetering on the edge.

I ask, "Did it always feel like the whole thing was going to explode in a fiery ball? That everyone was just barely holding on?"

He leans back against a boring marble countertop and says, "It did. There was this one time, I had some guys working for me that pushed the envelope. They decided they were going to have a party in this giant hotel suite so they come to me and say we're going to have a party. Before we even got there I realized this was going sideways. Every surf industry executive was there. They were all there. And my guys had these hookers come out and one is giving a guy a blow job in the middle of everyone, in the middle of fifty industry people, and he is going nuts and then her hair comes off in his hand. And it's a wig and she is completely bald. The whole place goes, 'Fuck! The chick's bald!' Everyone was horrified but that's what we were doing. That kind of stuff doesn't happen anymore. If something does happen, it is so locked up. Everything is so punitive, so confined, so restrictive. Back then it was all fun, though. Society wasn't all the way it was. Now it is so fucking conservative."

I nod too vigorously and reach for the bottle of Sancerre, filling my glass too full and spilling a bit but not caring because it is a small thing compared to pulling a hooker's wig off in the middle of an industry cocaine bash.

"So fucking conservative. But, why?" I ask. "The whole thing is circling the drain. Companies going bankrupt, mass layoffs, sales numbers through the floor. You'd think everyone would just give up, would do what they feel instead of doing what they think they should, or at least externally. There is more cocaine today, I think, or at least as much, but you never hear fun stories. It's only chatty, grindy, sweaty. It's never unhinged. Why not unhinge? It is the fucking apocalypse, after all."

Michael shakes his head slowly and pours his own self some more Sancerre.

"Exactly. But the thing is, you know, the Internet is so fucking cruel. I suffer from internet justice. I was beaten to a pulp on the fucking Internet for half a gram. It's another reason I moved here. Because everywhere I go in Laguna I'm so known in that town. I'm under a microscope there. It's a fucking joke. In San Clemente nobody knows me from fucking Adam. I've seen three cops since I've been here. There, in Laguna, they'd sit outside my house waiting for me to do something. It's a fucking joke. And they'd tell me they were doing that. So here is low-key. People just want to step on you. They get off on it somehow. I don't know why."

"But why drugs?" I press. "Why not stinginess or greed or sloth or pride or envy or any one of a hundred thousand different sins? Why cocaine?"

Michael looks defeated for the first time. Utterly worn out. "I don't fucking know."

"Are you running from it anymore?" I ask.

"Well not anymore," he says, slumping forward, away from the boring marble counter, back to the nondescript island. "I don't give a shit. What happened happened. So what. Sue me. I've already paid my price. It's cost me hundreds of thousands of dollars. And the people, yeah, they weigh in. It's time for Michael to clean up. Yeah, yeah, yeah. Until they come here, then they call me and say, 'Hey, do you have some?' It's like, don't try and put me into any kind of role model. Leave the model out. I'm just rolling. Where did I inherit that fucking responsibility? You wouldn't believe how deep-seated it is. I become the cathartic cleanse for them because they can say, 'Look how bad Michael Tomson is.' You know what I'm saying?"

The cathartic cleanse. Look how bad Michael Tomson is. I know exactly what he is saying and suddenly feel drained. Horribly miserable. We chat a little more about books, about William Finnegan's Pulitzer Prize-winning surf book *Barbarian Days*, which he calls "fucking great" but also says, "I read it closely twice for lack of authenticity and there are only two places. One is when he is writing and he is my age, sixty-two or sixty-three, and he writes about pulling into a double barrel in New York and I just put the book down and said, 'FUCK YOU! In your fucking dreams, Bill. Double barrel. Really.' We chat a little more about how he is going to his house on the North Shore tomorrow. About how there is an epic wave that breaks out in front of some property he owns but it is a pain in the ass to surf because Eddie Rothman is always changing the gate code locking him out. About the book he will someday write, but I can't concentrate on any of it. I feel like I'm getting sick. Like I'm sliding down the throat of a vicious, puking drunk, and it is not because of the Sancerre.

After an hour or so, I wish him *bon voyage*, tell him to hug Eddie for me, and limp into San Clemente's starry night feeling the worst. I came up to Michael Tomson's house imagining I was a great prophet. I wanted his stories, big and bold. I wanted the cocaine-fueled nights, a rock that could smash the chains of conservatism that strangles the very life out of surfing. I wanted to bring these to the people below and stand, still glowing a brilliant cocaine white from being in Michael Tomson's presence, on a stage made of broken surfboards and bellow, "Come, my children, and listen to a way for us to truly live again! I have been to San Clemente's mountaintop! I have the truth!"

But it absolutely smashed me hearing him talk about the weight of people's judgment, of their hypocrisy, of the sacrificial lamb he becomes for their personal senses of morality, that I was doing the same exact thing except flipped. I need Michael to be a party monster because I don't have the constitution to be one myself. I come from good Christian parents who refused to drink Australian beer and were internally hurt by mean-spiritedness in surf advertisements. I am an antisocial, generally quiet, introverted thing who is happiest in bed by 10:00 p.m. after three, or maybe four, vodka sodas and an episode of *Big Little Lies*, snuggled up next to my wife and daughter. I drag her to church each and every Sunday morning (even though her only real rule is snitches get stitches). I am not a party monster.

Oh, I know I'm not good. My ex-wife gave a recent interview in promotion of an album she was trying to Kickstart where I was described thusly: "He'd spent the past two years of their happy marriage fucking his barely legal-age student, that he sold the house they'd bought as newlyweds and kept the money, that he didn't even wait until their divorce was final to remarry and have a baby." And I've done enough cocaine to know that the feeling is exactly like surfing. A brain firing crescendo that almost instantly dissipates and leaves no memory.

I'm not good but I'm also not brave enough to do what society deems as really bad. I'm not bold enough to be Michael Tomson, so I need him to be Michael Tomson for me and to hell with the price— physical, financial, emotional, mental—that he has to pay.

I am an upside-down hypocrite and I slink to my Volkswagen Jetta Wagon feeling worse than I ever have in my entire life, or at least since Julie Briggs broke up with me. Way worse than when I got remarried and had a baby before officially being divorced or anything else I ever did to my ex-wife. I am a damned plaster sinner.

San Clemente's lights don't twinkle so brightly as I slink down the mountain. Everything feels sad and hollow. Everything feels hopeless and that's before I check my phone and see Ian Cairns, the father of the ASP, one-time Bronzed Aussie, has commented on my Facebook page underneath the story I had posted just hours earlier about *BeachGrit* sponsoring that riot in Huntington Beach. "Proposing a riot at HB at the US Open contest is stupid and lower than your normal gutter writing (I deleted journalism)." The words shine into my face. "Maybe we could get a little welcome panel together especially for *BeachGrit*...." And then he lists some names that I think are supposed to be threatening. And even though I respond, "Sounds great! Should I bring cake or maybe some Pepsi to this welcome panel party?" my heart is not into being an asshole because I really am an asshole. And not the useful kind.

Surf journalist. Fucking surf journalist. But I've even been demoted from that now, too, apparently. I'm just a simple gutter writer. I thought, for one all-too-brief moment, that I might have a special purpose. That I just could make surfing great again by bringing a story of undying love to the world. That it would be so grand as to unite *Duck Dynasty* and the Indigo Girls. That would be so magnificent as to end the surf industry apocalypse by launching today's youth back toward the brands so they could wear the rebellion. That they could wear freedom and the brilliant sun would shine again like it once did.

Gutter writer.

Fucking.

Gutter.

Writer.

12

Death of Dreams!

I have lost my velocity, sitting in front of a computer screen with the words "Help: Surf Icon vows rage!" staring back. I have lost my rhythm. In those early adventure days, running from Al-Qaeda in Yemen or Hezbollah in Lebanon or the Assads in Syria, it was always and ever about movement. Movement was the story. Velocity. It didn't matter why the movement was happening or where it was going. The only thing that mattered was never stopping.

Movement. Velocity. But I've stopped now. I'm stuck. Not moving and the curser blinks on my computer screen and inspiration, even for the easiest *BeachGrit* nothings that would typically be a slam dunk. Ian Cairns, the Bronzed Aussie, calling me a gutter writer? Adjectives, adverbs, and malapropisms should be gushing, but I've got nothing. I have run dry. Spent.

And then things spin downward still. An email pops up on my screen from Marcus Sanders, the editor of *Surfline*, the most trafficked website in all of surf. He is apparently angry over a picture we just used on *BeachGrit*'s Instagram. "It's our staff photographer's photo," he writes. "Please take it down." I explode into a ball of irrational rage and refuse, even though it would have been the kind thing to do, but I am furious. I am furious and exhausted of the pointless stillness.

There's nothing left. I am a living representation of the surf industry in the 1990s. A confused, tired, worn-out, stuck disaster.

The 1980's surf industry was such a pop. It was amazing. DayGlo, neon, Gotcha, if-you-don't-surf-don't-start dreams. Investors came, the companies grew and grew wildly, but "the dream" and "the bottom line" don't make happy bedfellows. The brands had to pump product into department stores and the new mall stores in order to keep growth alive, and as soon as the core surf shop kid saw the brands he loved in department stores and at the mall, as soon as he saw the kooks in school wearing what defined him, he left it behind.

Everything is cyclical in fashion and obviously cuts come and go and come. Colors come and go and come. Trends come and go and come. Pegged pants come and go and come. Surf came and went, but it is a difficult thing for true surfers to understand because why would anyone ever leave surf? True surfers, including those that staff the surf industry, are caught off guard by each recession because surf is the only thing in the world that makes sense to them and when the public writ large catches on for brief moments, they agitate at the potential crowds in the water but also, quietly, feel that they are the secret kings of the entire world. The envy of civilization. But when it goes out, surfers are never prepared, or at least those who make their money in surf.

The professional surfing tour, dreamt up by Fred Hemmings and executed more properly by Ian Cairns, had expanded to a thousand shitty little beach breaks with professionals mastering the art of "three turns to the beach." The ugliest sort of anything, where the most talented of surfers grovel for points. Bumping and jiving. Bouncing and hopping in waves that even the most desperate kids frown upon. It is an entirely unattractive dance, even to the most diehard surf fan, and turned off any potential newcomers.

Furthermore, by 1990, surfing was officially old. Three full generations had sucked the marrow. Grandparents were riding the longboards Michael Tomson detested. Lawyer dads were out shredding dawn patrol. Doctor moms were wearing Quiksilver's new Roxy and catching the evening glass-off with their girlfriends. Surfing, for maybe the first time in its history, was totally and completely lame. A giant turkey trot.

It wasn't all bad, of course. Kelly Slater turned pro in 1990. The bronzed, half-Syrian wunderkind from Cocoa Beach, Florida, may be the greatest figurehead any sport/industry/activity has ever had. A smidge better than Muhammad Ali. One hundred times better than Lance Armstrong. He has miraculously remained beyond handsome and beyond talented for almost fifty years, winning eleven world titles and costarring on *Baywatch*. He has also dated Leonardo DiCaprio's girlfriend (Bar Refaeli), Tom Brady's wife (Gisele Bündchen), Justin Timberlake's ex (Cameron Diaz), and Pamela Anderson. How is that?

The year 1990 was also the year Tom Carroll entered the Australian Surfing Hall of Fame. The short, powerful man from Sydney dominated the tours in the 1980s and always seemed a clean-cut poster child for hard work and good living. He even wore a helmet when surfing Pipeline. The best example possible for young impressionable kids.

In the 2000s, he helped push big-wave surfing to new heights by towing into never-before-witnessed monsters, a thing that over-the-hill surfers do even today. I was never too much a fan, since he is short and powerful and also since he surfed big waves, but after his competitive days were over, his brother Nick, the most famous surf journalist of all, wrote a biography detailing how much cocaine Tom had stuffed up his nose and it made me like him lots more.

Still, outside of Kelly and outside of Tom's addiction, things were grim. The 1980s and the yuppies and the fun had taken a real toll. Stockbrokers were going to see psychiatrists, complaining about strange visions and uncontrollable paranoia—not quite as fantastic as David Bowie's semen-stealing demons, perhaps, but still enough to drive them to seek help.

The first batch of help-seekers was turned away because cocaine still wasn't seen as addictive in those early years. But then John Belushi died of an overdose, Richard Pryor set himself on fire freebasing it, crack got invented, and Ronald Reagan decided that better than the wars in Afghanistan and South America was to ramp up America's war on drugs by enforcing mandatory minimum sentencing and locking kids up for decades. Crack was more heavily punished than cocaine because it was an inner-city drug, not a trading-floor surf one, but in broad culture the sheen had worn off.

Cocaine shifted away from being Dom Pérignon to being the thing responsible for crack babies, riots, murders, and celebrity death. Like surfing, it was out of style. Stuck in the quicksand of changing taste. It was out. Hammered. Done. Except in a surf culture that was circling the drain of relevancy just like it is today.

And I'm stuck in the quicksand of my own moral quagmire which my computer is mocking with its hypocritical cursor. On off. On off. Not being one nor the other. Being false. Blink.

Blink.

Blink.

With blank spaces on either side. Blank spaces. Nothing. Nothing but "Help: Surf icon vows rage!" I can't even muster the strength to be a gutter writer anymore. Knowing that I'm an upside-down hypocrite has finally killed me all the way, or at least killed what is left of my completely compromised aspirations.

The sun is shining and the birds are chirping. I log on to *Surfline* just to get away from the cursor and to see what is happening in the water even though it means that damned Marcus Sanders gets my click. It's calling 3-5 occ. 6 "Primary/peaking WNW swell blends with some smaller SSW swell this morning. Many spots throughout the region offer broken-up and fairly peaky, waist-, shoulder-high surf with occasional head-high sets."

Basically gibberish. *Surfline* only speaks nonsense, so much nonsense that some amazing woman just tattooed "Fuck *Surfline*" on her heel. Can you imagine the frustration that it would take to do that? Fuck *Surfline*, but from the accompanying web cam I can see it's good or at least fun, and fuck it. Fuck it all. I push away from my desk and the cursor and the molasses surrounding my life, go to the garage, grab my board, throw it in my Volkswagen Jetta Wagon, and coast down the hill to the beach.

It is a brilliant day. The sun glistening in a cornflower sky. The smallest touch of warm wind tickling the palms but not rippling the water. The smell of *carne asada* and s'mores floating. Good-sized set waves stacking out the back, mowing over a couple on matching foam Costco Wavestorms. They are paddling furiously and appear to be shouting encouragement to one another as the militant whitewash steams in then swamps them, their Costco Wavestorms shooting into the air. Tangling and dragging owners.

Otherwise it is not too crowded and I hop down the stairs, two at a time, happy to leave the world, my purpose, my stalled journey behind. Happy to vacate my last few drips of sense. It is what all surfers do, I suppose. Surfing becomes an unconscious tic, like Tourette's, and so when the mind stops functioning properly the surfer automatically just goes surfing. It's another reason that Hollywood has never figured out how to make a proper surf film. The directors and producers and actors who don't have pterygium actually push through creative blocks and get things done instead of fleeing into the ocean and pretending to dance. There is no such thing as a successful surfer, outside the professional tour or the industry. President Obama? He didn't surf. He swam in the ocean. Eddie Vedder? Nope, he rides egg-shaped things. Matthew McConaughey? Yeah, he's not a real surfer. Chris Hemsworth? He might become a proper actor and win all the Academy Awards on offer if he just stopped fucking surfing. Scott Caan? Three words: *Hawaii. Five. 0.*

And I plunge into the cool Pacific, feeling the sun on my shoulders, the salt water in my hair, and don't care about any of it, wondering if this is how Jonah felt when he jumped overboard.

I paddle to the lineup easily enough, duck-diving a good set wave and watching the white clouds of aerated water boil and churn over my head. A good duck dive feels almost as good as a proper wave. Gliding beneath the ferocity of the ocean.

It feels good, right, and I sit on my board, alternately squirting water through my hands and shielding my eyes, looking out toward the horizon. Listening to the surfers around me talk about upcoming trips to Indonesia and Mexico. About waves they just came back from in Costa Rica and New Zealand. It really is a wonder that surfers, as shallow and empty as we are, travel so wide and far for waves. I think of all the places I've been for waves and think that the act of surfing, in and of itself, is velocity.

And like that, a wave comes. I am not in the right place but think about dropping in anyway because I am frustrated and surf-starved, but better judgment carries the day and I watch a tanned youth shimmy off the bottom and rocket down the line right underneath my nose. He is the very picture of cool, of surf perfection, and he moves.

Another wave comes, and this time I do drop in because I see the unfortunate man wearing earplugs and riding an ugly seven-foot epoxy thing from Thailand that is not going to make it. I keep my eyes on him, watch his knee pummel the deck of his board, watch his hand slip off the rail, watch him bury in the wave, becoming one with it, and he moves.

I pop up and imagine that I look like a graceful pelican as I glide up and down before cutting back and rebounding off the whitewash. Moving. I am happy Earplugs fell and might have internally mocked his inability but know better because even though I imagine I look like a graceful pelican, in reality I'm somewhere between a limping gazelle and an injured drop bear. I have seen the proof.

It happened during a fine enough day just recently and I was out shredding. Killing it. Radical turns off the top. Committed bottom turns with a totally engaged rail. I caught one last one, whacked it off the lip then rode the whitewash in, feeling like Mikhail Baryshnikov. Like Aleksandr fucking Petrovsky.

A woman was standing on the cliff, near the path toward the street with a camera, and she smiled at me as I approached on my way up. "I got some shots of you today…" she said with coy eyes.

"Yeah?" I responded, and she handed me a business card that said, "You were shredding! I got the proof!" with a web address where her pictures could be purchased.

I gave her a cool guy thanks while maybe tossing a very lazy shaka, took the card, and went about my day. That night, though, after a few vodka drinks, I got curious and logged on to her site, scrolled through the day's pictures, and found three of me. My radical turns off the top looked like a giraffe on ice skates. My committed bottom turns looked like a three-year-old trying to sink a toy boat in the bathtub. My whack off the lip was not actually off the lip but midway through a wave that was no bigger than knee high. It was embarrassing. It's always embarrassing for anyone but pros or ex-pros to see themselves surf. The chasm between what we imagine and what we are is vast but instantly bridged with photo or video evidence in a deeply troubling way. What we imagine is poetic, and what we are is fucked, but both cases are movement. Both are velocity. And as I paddle back out to the lineup, I feel as though I'm coming unstuck. That I'm starting to break through.

And this is also the problem with surfing as Tourette's. With surfing becoming an unconscious tic. The stuck surfer always feels like he reaches some sort of breakthrough when he gets out in the water. I know it is impossible, but I would love to see the actual quality of ideas had while surfing. I bet they are almost as good as the ideas had while high on weed: a little worse than the problems solved with cocaine.

But still, I'm feeling it. My mind is racing again. Clarity beginning to rise from the grave where my completely compromised aspirations had just been buried. A renewed sense of purpose starting to pulse through my veins as I feel the waves start to dissipate in my body, and I watch as Earplugs paddles while lying too far back on his board and the tanned youth attempting air reverse after air reverse and the cool kids and the rad dad and the world travelers.

When I first started doing surf journalism, splashing in the shallow end, contextualizing the nothing, writing for the audience I'm amongst right now, I made a name for myself by being the most decadent surf journalist around. For only writing about sex, sex, drugs, drugs, and maybe, if there was no more sex or drugs or drugs, then writing about surfing. I wasn't very popular. Letters to the editor, comment boards, social media posts would all decry my particular brand of what my best Australian pal and biz partner deemed "trash prose," but I didn't give two shits. That was the surf world as I saw it. Cocaine and meaningless sex. Those were the two things everyone appreciated equally.

And if everyone is going to live that way, then they should embrace it. What is the point of racking rails and mindlessly rooting chicks if you are going to pretend you aren't? Martin Luther, one of the greatest Christians of all time, wrote, "Be a sinner and sin boldly, but believe and rejoice in Christ more boldly still." In my mind the two are the same and all I wanted the surf industry, the surfers, the hangers-on to do was to be bold and sin boldly. To not hide anymore. To exit the closet into the full warm light of grace. To set out on the path that will end with them believing and rejoicing in Christ more boldly still. Right?

I was allowed to edit an issue of a surf magazine one time in my life. Australia's *Stab*. The fake version of *BeachGrit*. And I agreed as long as I could put an Australian star surfer on the cover with his whole head buried in a second-place trophy filled with cocaine. The owner, a striking blonde man who wore purple Gucci high-tops, hemmed and hawed, trying to get me off the idea in a multitude of ways before finally saying no. So I agreed to edit the issue if I could sublimate a swastika over a picture of a man riding a gorgeous wave while the sun set on the cover instead. He let me. And how crazy is that? How fucking crazy is that? Cocaine-addled surfers are more afraid of cocaine depictions than they are of being likened to Nazi Germany.

Wild.

The cover bit that owner on his ass when Australian surf hero Mick Fanning called me a "fucking Jew" at his world title party. I wrote a story detailing the funny exchange but Mick did not think it was funny and went crying to the press, insisting I was the anti-Semite because I stuck swastikas on magazine covers. Every one of those back issues quickly disappeared.

But, oh, that was a fun dance, and fuck Mick Fanning to this day. He deserves to get eaten by a shark, which he almost did get in South Africa, but whatever. Sin and sin boldly! That's what I want all surfers to do. That's what Michael Tomson did, and I'm not an upside-down hypocrite for appreciating him, for thinking he is the pinnacle of our surf world. I can't walk his path, but I can still carry his story, and it will free Earplugs and the tanned youth and the cool kids and the rad dads, even the damned skintight polo dads from their lame bondage. What is more, I can just tell the truth. Why fucking not? It's the apocalypse—who's gonna bust me?

I take the next wave in and run across the sand, back up the steps, two at a time, excited to get back to my computer. Excited to move this love story along. I fish my car keys out of some nearby bushes, pop the back, throw my board in, and skip to the driver's door, checking my phone just to make sure my cute little button of a daughter didn't call someone an asshole again at school, but there's another text message from an unknown Orange County number.

"Hey, Chad. Got your number from Matt. If you're really doing a story on what I think you're doing a story on then we need to talk."

I read it twice. Fucking Chad. "Chas" always gets spell-check corrected into "Chad" and it drives me crazy. I really, really don't like the name Chad but I guess it is my punishment for going by Chas publically. My penance for actively pushing a totally douche nickname. Chas. Have you ever met a Chas who wasn't a douche? Exactly.

But the meat of the text. Who is it from and what does he have to tell me? Part of me is very curious. Part of me dreads. After cocaine and meaningless sex, surfers love telling stories most of all. Surf historian Matt Warshaw wrote that he "couldn't wait to sledge away at the cheerleading and boosterism and perjured nobility layered onto most of the surf history. Pulling down shoddy historiographic handicraft is, by itself, I admit, pretty satisfying." Oh Lord! I can't even imagine the stories he had to sit through while writing his masterpiece. Surfers will drop names and then more names and then more and more and more names.

Like, "There was this one time where Dougie Freeburn and Finless Frankie were out at North Point and Jock paddled out on his nine-zero and Dougie said, 'What the hell is that?' but Jock thought he said, 'Could I smell your hat?' and that is where the term 'evening glass' came from."

Or, "Disco Dave was ripping out at Swami's and watched a dolphin jump out of the water, and this was in nineteen-seventy-four, so he wanted to try it to and this is where surf wax came from…"

Or…never mind. I will spare you.

It is one of the more difficult parts of surf journalism, if any of it can actually be described as "difficult," figuring out how to cut every story but a few. Shredding characters and episodes and stories that all mean something and point to something, but fucking hell it is easy to lose the main track and end up in some weird narrative backwater holding Finless Frankie's hand in weeds so tall that they block out the sun.

And I'm hoping beyond fucking hope that these are not the weeds when I text back, "Sure! Where you wanna meet?" I had just regained velocity, even if it was only an illusion. I was about to move again but now I guess I'm moving to…and my phone buzzes a text response.

"San Juan Capistrano? There's that little bistro by the train tracks."

I'm moving to Orange County. Back to cocaine's adopted home.

Son of a bitch. But was there ever really another way?

13

The Magic Flight!

A train blows its whistle as it comes into the station, startling me from a story about where the swallows went. They were what once made San Juan Capistrano famous, flying up from Argentina on March 19 of each and every year and nesting in the town's famous mission. Pat Boone sang about them. So did Elvis Presley. "When the swallows come back to Capistrano," they crooned, "that's the day you promised to come back to me. When you whispered, 'Farewell,' in Capistrano, 'twas the day the swallow flew out to sea."

Ha! Schlocky bullshit, but guess who hasn't come back to Capistrano since 2009? Pat Boone, he's too busy being old and accusing Obama of being a Muslim. Elvis, he's too busy being dead. And the swallows? They're too busy building nests in the dung of Chino Hills instead of San Juan. An inland city famous for cows and Steve McQueen attending its high school for troubled boys. And so San Juan Capistrano is now famous for nothing. For nothing but memories of fabulous times past.

And no one knows why the sparrows left, I was reading before the train blew its whistle. Some think that it is because of a building tossed up taller than the mission in 2009 and it threw the birds off their migratory game. Some think the birds really never actually returned, en masse, to Capistrano, that it was only folklore pushed out by Pat

Boone and Elvis Presley. Others think that the California urban sprawl disoriented the birds. Or at least those are the three theories kicked out by the *Los Angeles Times* in its 2009 story. It almost reads like a *BeachGrit* story and I'm about to make a mental note to employ it as a story intro when I hear a "Chaaaaaas…" and look up and see Jeffrey Lebowski.

Not the rich one in the wheelchair, but The Dude. The Jeff Bridges one. The Dude in gait, The Dude in movement. The Dude in dress. The Dude in everything but White Russian. And as I wonder what stories of 1970s cocaine smuggling he is going to get me in the weeds over, my heart sinks. Fuck. The damned weeds. Even worse if he thinks this love story is actually about weed. Oh, please no. Please, please, please, no. Weed stories are the absolute worst.

The Dude reaches out his hand and says, "I'm Jim Zapala. Nice to meet you, man…" and he totally sounds like The Dude, too. Like he fell out of the movie and into San Juan Capistrano.

"Nice to meet you too," I respond with a sinking pit in my stomach. The velocity I had just grabbed by the tail, even if it is totally illusionary, will definitely be undone if Jim gets into weed stories. Fuck.

"We can grab a drink or something to eat right over here, man," he says, pointing to a woodsy outdoor patio attached to a cute bistro.

Bistro. I never eat at "bistros" and I think it is a subconscious tic stemming from my Coos Bay roots. There was a bistro down near the tugboat dock and my dad told me it was owned by an atheist who didn't support Coos Bay schools because he voted no on some school funding measure and they served beer and wine. That was three strikes right there, and I suppose, my heart still retains a beat of revulsion against the bistro.

These dens of unmitigated sin.

These degraded hovels that don't support public education.

But this one is cute and maybe I should rethink the bistro program. We sit at a high outdoor table, I order a vodka soda, Jim orders a shrimp ceviche that he pronounces "civeechi." "I'll take the civeechi, man…" and then he looks at me and says, "Are you really doing a story on surfing and drugs?"

I look him up and down and say, "No. Not drugs. Cocaine. Only cocaine."

He leans back like The Dude, eyes smiling, mouth pulling into a broad grin, and starts vigorously shaking his head up and down in agreement. Like he has been waiting for this moment his whole life. Waiting for someone to see that all the weed and LSD and heroin and pills and whatever are all cheap and meaningless nothings. That surfing and cocaine are the only true lovers. A story that transcends. And he says, "That IS the drug. That's it. It is cocaine. As much as it was then it is today. And I've done so much and so has everyone else. Throughout those years there is not one president, well, there were a few exceptions like Bob Hurley and—I don't know, a few others, but, man, it was everywhere and it's still around today as much as it was then. Cocaine. It's cocaine."

My drink arrives. I take a long sip, keeping Jim in my gaze, and all of a sudden I get the overwhelming feeling that this meeting was written in the stars. Ordained by God. Maybe. I ask him, "So what is your hook in this damned little surf industry of ours?"

He leans forward and says, "MT, man."

In the normal course of my surf journalism duties, I usually relegate the chore of corroborating stories to the pile of things that will not get done that day—mixed right in with smogging the car and putting the bedroom curtains up. There is rarely a point in my mind. Surfing, surf personalities, and surf stories are about a sensation. Whether any of it is true or not is immaterial and doesn't change the way it feels. Except truth matters in love. Truth and honesty may even matter more than anything else. True love cannot exist, much less grow, where falsehoods flourish. Where lies or omissions strangle. God knew that I would take Michael Tomson's stories, his value, his importance at face value so he brought me an angel dressed like The Dude.

Maybe.

"You worked for Gotcha?" I ask.

"Yeah, man, so this would have been in nineteen eighty-eight or eighty-nine, that's when I started doing work for them, and they were the kings. They were doing probably one hundred twenty-five million a year, which, for that time, was unheard of. Being from Newport, all my friends worked at Quiksilver, but Gotcha was in its heyday at that moment. So I went and met MT. He gave me a T-shirt to do a graphic on so I did it for him and I brought it to him and, you know, he was *the* guy so I brought it and he said, 'Okay. You want a job?' And so here I'm twenty-eight years old. He offered me a job as a clothing designer and I didn't have any training or anything and I said, 'Well shit.' Gotcha was the coolest thing in the world back then and at that time it was huge. I think the M+D department had, like, forty-five people. It was giant and I was just so in awe. I literally didn't speak in that building for two years because I was so…I wanted to learn everything. Everyone was great and it was such a good time."

His civeechi comes and he deftly snags a shrimp with a chip. It's almost hard to imagine the surf industry being the coolest thing in the world, huge and vibrant. The predominate sensation when walking into the headquarters of Quiksilver, Billabong, Rip Curl, Reef, Volcom, Hurley, etc., today is sadness. It's desperation, which is quickly chased by lots of marketing speak.

"How was working for Michael?" I ask. I'd heard a few different stories before and most weren't the best.

Jim snags another shrimp and says, "You know, I've worked for a lot of guys…Michael was…" and he pauses looking over my shoulder, searching for words. "You could call him any time of the night and say, 'I've got an idea or this or that,' and he was the most supportive ever. He'd always be up for it. He'd be like, 'Do it! Let's do it!' Most inspirational guy I've ever seen. He just completely loved and had a passion for creativity and wanted to do whatever. If it felt good, let's fucking do it."

Again, I'm struck by the dissonance bouncing off today's surf industry where, aside from inventing anti-shark technology that gets kids' arms bitten off, genius is in short supply and creativity in even shorter.

"Not only was he the most inspirational person to be around," Jim continues, "but what I really saw in him was his ability to see stuff way down the road. And that blew me away. I can't think what

I'm going to do in the next two hours. He has such perception of what is going to happen."

And this almost seamless corroboration with how Michael perceives his own particular abilities makes me wonder. How often do our perceptions about what makes us great, or at least unique, line up with what others think makes us unique or at least tolerable? I've always cherished my ability to link two seemingly disparate concepts together, demonstrating the undeniable connection between things that should never touch. I latched on to the dreamy idea of California and its embodiment in surfing when I was a boy and mashed the two together in Oregon. I accidentally studied for a semester at Oxford University's Keble College when I was an undergraduate in a renaissance and medieval studies program. We were supposed to read and expound on a ménage of Shakespeare in the 1590s and Constantine's vision of warfare and Plato's influence on Machiavelli. All fine and good, but I discovered Albert Camus in Oxford and couldn't get enough. When I was supposed to be reading the mystics, I was reading *The Plague* and *The Stranger* and *The Myth of Sisyphus* underneath those soaring spires. When the semester ended, we were supposed to write some massive thesis, and I wrote about how Camus was a modern version of St. Bonaventure. I was the only student in the entire program to get a D. But I didn't care, because then I started traveling to the Middle East feeling in my heart of hearts that radical Islam was the new punk rock. All those early stories pushed this narrative. That radical Islam was nothing to fear. That it was the only young and viable alternative discourse alive in a world overcome by knee-jerk capitalism. Hezbollah might have given me a D, too, but I didn't care because I was surfing again. Watching cocaine disappear up noses and just beginning to feel the pangs of the world's greatest love story.

Does anyone else appreciate this in me? I will tell you now: No.

My links seem arbitrary and fall apart under the withering stares of high school girlfriends, scholars, and jihadis. Except this last one between cocaine and surfing will not fall apart because the surf industry has no withering stare and more importantly because it is true.

But cocaine. I almost forgot about cocaine and ask Jim, "But what about cocaine? What about Michael and his legendary cocaine?"

Jim rubs his chin and says, "Hmmmm. Man, nobody was ever like Michael. When I first started going there he was beginning to become distant from the company. He would show up at eleven forty-five and he would leave at one forty-five and nobody would see him. He had a private entrance. And Joel, his partner, we didn't talk to him. Joel was the cheesiest guy in the world. Michael was the pro surfer, good-looking guy. Joel didn't surf, wore parachute pants and silk Gucci shirts unbuttoned and medallions. And fuck! So the company was split in half. You had marketing and design, which was Michael's. Joel was sales and production. So it was like two completely different companies. Like, we were fucking cool, and they were cheeseballs. I never even talked to Joel. He was just so ewww. So Michael was becoming—here's a good story for you.

"We threw this party once and Michael wasn't there but this was the ethos of the time, right. Blow and craziness and, like, the best time ever. So the good thing was, I had a real job, and for the first time I thought, 'Fuck, I could do this.' Not that I was worried, I was having the time of my life, but all of a sudden, at that time, I mean…It was at the height. All of a sudden I'm flying first class on Virgin to London and Paris and told 'buy whatever the fuck you want' and staying at the best hotels and it was just insane. But one of the things I'll remember at the very first sales meeting I went into, it was at the Phoenician Resort in Arizona so we had this sales meeting and we fly there, check in, and I remember the lobby was giant and all these tourists were there, fat people from Minneapolis and they were all wearing Gotcha. I thought, 'This company is even more popular than I ever imagined. Even tourists were wearing Gotcha!' Everybody in the lobby. Neon orange and lime and Gotcha everywhere. I thought, 'Shit. This is the biggest company in the world.'

"The next day we go into this huge ballroom and all those people I thought were tourists wearing Gotcha were the sales force. And there were hundreds of them. That's when I figured out, that was the demise. Michael was becoming more and more reclusive and Joel couldn't say no to a deal. All these sleazeballs were selling it and that was the end. I didn't know it, though, and neither did anyone else because when you're going up you don't think about going down. And Gotcha was one of the first to go that way, but I've seen companies make the exact same mistakes for the last thirty years. Let's get a new building, let's acquire. Acting like the party is never going to end. It just got sleazier and sleazier. And that's why we started More Core Division in 1990 or maybe 1991, because Michael wanted to have his identity back. Good business. He didn't start MCD because Gotcha was going south. He just wanted to get back to his core customer. The specialty stores turned on Gotcha. Nobody liked Joel, and he became the face of the company. Michael became more reclusive. You know the surf industry guys who succeeded in those years knew it was important to sustain those relationships but Michael was just getting more and more into his weird world. He started not wanting to be around Gotcha, to be around those people, the product was changing, we had kind of a recession there that really hit the wall in ninety, ninety-one. A lot of stuff started changing rapidly."

"Yeah sure, but the cocaine? What about the cocaine?"

Jim laughs. "I've been through a lot with Michael, I mean so much. We used to fly, back in the day, one time we went to Tavarua with a bunch of guys and this is when Michael was—there's no coke on Tavarua. So we fly to Hawaii then fly to Fiji then boat to Tavarua, and Cloudbreak was four- to six-foot the first three days. Just perfect. Just beautiful. The fourth day we wake up and Michael had to leave. He couldn't stay. He had to fly back to Hawaii because he couldn't be without his coke. It was as good as you'd want it to be in Tavarua, and he had to leave. The guy was just a freak coke addict, you know. He shouldn't be walking."

I drain my drink and order another while The Dude gets back into full rhythm.

"In the nineties when we were traveling, when he was going to London or Paris, he would Fed-Ex himself, in a magazine, a baggie of coke. And he would send it before we left and we'd be checking every day when we got back to the hotel from shopping. Half the time it wouldn't come but half the time it would and that was before Nine Eleven and all that, but we'd have great times in Paris when it'd show up.

"This one night we were in Paris, we had this guy who repped it in Europe and went out to this wild club. Michael left like he always did. I stayed, took a cab back to the hotel, and there were these two chicks out there asking if I wanted a massage. I'm going no, no, no. They were kind of…ugh. But I noticed they had a shopping bag that was from one of the stores me and Michael had bought stuff from that day and she is holding this bag and I'm thinking, 'That's weird, we bought stuff from that store.' I didn't think nothing of it. Went to bed. Saw Michael in the morning and he said, 'You wouldn't believe what happened to me last night. Two chicks asked if I wanted a massage. I said, "Yeah! Come up to the room!"' They came up to the room, the chicks are massaging him, he falls asleep and the chicks rip him off. He's running down the hall naked after them…" And Jim breaks into a wide laugh. "Stuff like that happened all the time."

He goes on and on in the most candid manner telling story after story of Gotcha mayhem, of Michael leading the charge. He tells the same story that Michael told about the hooker with the wig except in Jim's version it got ripped off in the bathroom, but still, the entire surf industry hierarchy, except Michael, was stuffed in there. Standing around the sinks and between the partitions. He tells stories of the darker side, employees that fell over the edge. "Man, we were amateurs when it came to partying when this all started, but we went gnarly. Or a lot of us did." He tells stories leading up to the present moment and Michael's legal trouble. "Michael was in very big denial when he started having legal problems. 'It's not my coke' and all that, and fuck that. Come on, Michael. But any one of the presidents of any of the companies. All of them were the same way. Michael just went bigger."

And he tells the stories with neither axe to grind nor conspiratorial attempt to tarnish anyone's reputation. He tells them without any particular relish. Without looking for any kind of rubberneck credit for exposing what would normally be considered unseemly bits. He loves Michael still and mostly tells the stories simply because they are true but also to highlight Michael's generosity.

"I think I know Michael more than anyone, and through everything, through my divorce. Michael called me and said, 'Hey, you're coming to Hawaii. Bought you a ticket. Come stay with me in Hawaii.' People don't realize how generous he is. I know all those guys. There is nobody like him. His generosity is…for all his other stuff…and that's the thing. Everybody turned on him but he was giving everybody coke. Everybody was partying on his dime. And those same people who are badmouthing him now or don't want to be around him now, they were right there with him, trust me. I was right there with him, too."

He sits back and stares at his half-eaten civeechi for a moment, lost in thought. Struggling under the weight of a clear and particular sadness.

"He is a very generous soul, man. He's got something. I know. I've seen him. He gave one surf industry executive eighty-K to get a house when that guy first moved here, to give him a start. He never paid him back. The guy has literally given away everything. For his drug demons, and they're there…"

He pauses again.

"I always knew the ride that he was on was not going to end well. He wasn't going to have any friends left because he was so powerful. The girls loved him, everybody loved the blow, they loved his power. I just knew you can't live this way and he is going to end up with nothing and nobody. Fuck. The surf industry, it's such a piece of shit. It's gotta be torn down and built from the bottom up. It's full of a bunch of shitheads and it has gotten more and more like that over the years. Bunch of fucking…"

He pauses for the last time.

"It'll never be like Michael Tomson again."

And with that, he pushes his chair back and wanders back from whence he came. Into an Orange County late afternoon. The rapidly disappearing sun bathing everything in the most golden light imaginable. I sit by myself for a long time, listening to the birds that aren't swallows chirping, watching the trains slow as they come into the station, disgorging business commuters, kids, and parents. Seeing a man in a teal Vissla T-shirt have a very animated conversation with a man in a Billabong T-shirt celebrating Billabong team rider Joel Parkinson's 2012 World Title. It screams "Parko!" in bold yellow font. And I wonder what they are discussing so passionately. Paul Naude, the man who held the United States' Billabong license forever had jumped ship a few years ago to start Vissla. Could they be arguing about surf industry ethics? About right and wrong?

14

Rescue from Without!

I spend the next few days wrestling with the meaning of cocaine and surfing in a deeper way, or at least deeper for me. Or at least more seriously. Not thinking about it in some grand arcing narrative. Not thinking about it as the oldest love story on earth or a great uniter of disparate communities in our completely fractured modern times. Not thinking of myself as surf journalist or narc or prophet or gutter writer or failure. Not thinking of myself at all, in fact, but thinking about generosity and honesty and how much I miss both. What the fuck happened? Where did they go? *Why* did they go?

My head is so clouded that I almost accidentally lose my daughter in Legoland's Adventure Club somewhere between the Ancient Egypt scene and the Ice Age one. I almost accidentally post a story on *BeachGrit* about how easily agitated surf photographers get, which would have fucked the website, literally, forever. Hell hath no fury like a surf photographer scorned, or so the old adage goes.

And now I'm at yet another surf film premiere, this one for a big-wave surfer who is nice enough, but I cannot be bothered with his general aesthetic and cannot be bothered with the empty surf chatter and cannot be bothered with the clenched jaws and un-drunk drinks because there is no love story on earth that is not generous and honest. And fuck. Where did they go? Why did generosity and honesty go?

This particular big-wave surf film is sponsored by Austria's number one export, Red Bull, which has tried to capture the "extreme sport" market since its inception with varying degrees of success, and it is a classic of its genre. Expensive. Super high-definition. Lots of very slow slo-mo. Some attempt at introspection. Generally unpopular. But Red Bull knows how to throw a party, and I am forever indebted. I met my wife while directing a Red Bull surf film at the premiere of a different Red Bull surf film. And what are the odds of that? In "extreme sport" they are actually pretty good.

I was living in Australia at the time and happy having just left the ex-wife, feeling free. The sun was bright, if cancerous, the meat pies were delicious, and I had a wonderful girlfriend in Melbourne. Then, out of the blue, professional Hawaiian surfer Jamie O'Brien called me and asked if I could come back to the States to direct his Red Bull film. He had all the footage, he just needed someone to put it together and tell a story. I told him yes on one condition: That I could go back to Australia in three weeks. He agreed and I flew to Los Angeles.

The second night I was back, professional surfer Julian Wilson premiered his Red Bull film in Santa Ana and I went to the premiere so I could gauge the state of the union. It was a fine film but nothing overwhelming, and I thought, "Oh yeah. Three weeks. I've got this." After it was done, I milled under the Orange County stars with the rest of the surf industry, feeling happy and good, and then the only surf film director worth anything, a true auteur who left Ridley Scott behind so that he could shoot surfers on film, a man named Joe G., came over to me, pointed to a gorgeous blonde across the patio, and said, "You and she are going to do amazing things together." He went, grabbed her by the arm, and within two months I was a bigamist with an Australian girlfriend. All thanks to Red Bull.

The energy drink giant was first introduced into the American market—via California, of course—in 1997. Right when the surf industry was ready to slough off its latest recession. Right when the world was beginning to gag for surf culture once again.

The stale 1990s, the demise of Gotcha and Op and the surf look, took a heavy toll, but the cancerous sun always shines again.

Kelly Slater with his girlfriends and his *Baywatch* kept getting more and more dreamy. Not only was he winning every surf contest, rising up the ranks and winning world titles, he was on the cover of Andy Warhol's *Interview Magazine* under the brilliant headline "Half Fish, Total Dish!" And he was the best thing to happen to surfing since Peruvians and cocaine, but he wasn't the only sexy thing happening.

Lisa Andersen, my favorite surfer ever, was winning her own titles and so sexy, so cute, so stylish, so good on a surfboard that Quiksilver invented a whole line for her. Roxy took the world by storm. Every girl wanted to be a Roxy girl, and every girl wanted to own a pair of Roxy board shorts. All of a sudden they could have something in the surf world that wasn't purely demeaning. That was forward-looking, fun, and proudly feminine. Lisa Andersen was a better representation of the surf ideal than had ever existed before. Even better than Kelly Slater. She was tan, fit, wildly talented, and delightfully sexy. She was surf and a mini-revolution followed in her caramel wake.

Even better, the film *Blue Crush* came out, which featured girl surfers conquering Oahu's North Shore. It was inspirational, even though it was made, written, and directed by Hollywood folk who don't even know what pterygia are, much less have them. Even though the waves were actually ridden by stuntmen in drag. The film displayed a world of surf sexy that had been sorely missing and made a cool $52 million at the box office.

Brian Grazer produced it, and I think he maybe thinks he's a surfer. Like rips Malibu and Hawaii. I lunched with him once in his Hollywood office and he asked me if the G-UNIT box of clothes that just came in was cool. Even better, though, and Michael Tomson told me this story, one time he and Eddie Rothman were apparently shopping at Foodland on the North Shore, filling up their cart with booze and meat. When it was time to check out, Eddie patted his back pocket and said, "Brah. I forgot my wallet."

Michael patted his back pocket and said, "Bruh. I forgot mine too."

Eddie scanned the people in line and said, "No problem. See dat guy with the hair all sticking up? He wants to do my life story. We'll make him pay for it."

It was Brian Grazer, and as the story goes, he whipped out his wallet faster than you can say "false crack" and eagerly bought Eddie Rothman and Michael Tomson all of their groceries. Eddie laughed as the two left and said, "He ain't never gonna do my life story."

Very funny.

And while Brian Grazer may never get to make *Ho Braddah: An Eddie Rothman Life,* his *Blue Crush* was genuinely okay. The girls had cracked a new market and Laird Hamilton, on the other end of the sexuality spectrum, had just come into his own. The adopted son of Bill Hamilton, 1970s surf-style master, was so much man he'd make Hercules weep with envy. Six foot three and cut from marble with a neck as thick as a redwood and a jaw like a bulldozer. He decided that the tiny little beach-break waves on that day's professional tour were not conducive to his girth, so he struck out on his own to conquer the biggest monsters the ocean could serve up.

In an odd turn, he too jumped into weird surf Hollywood, starring as the bad guy in the surf schlock classic *North Shore* with neon paint swirling around his nipples. His poor acting did little to damage his big-wave skill, though, and it was Laird's ride at a newly hyped Tahitian spot named Teahupo'o that kicked both him, and surfing, to the next level. Teahupo'o translates to English as "to sever the head" or "place of crushed skulls" and a better description could not be painted. It is a scary wave, coming out of the deep and breaking on a shallow shelf. It is like the ocean folds over on itself, thundering and groaning.

Laird's wave, caught in 2000 and dubbed "The Millennium Wave," was a massive thing. A behemoth that sucked off the reef and stacked up, blocking out the sun, thicker than his neck, than a whole redwood forest. Heavier than André the Giant. He got towed in, thighs flexing underneath the curtain smack dab in the heat of the wave. It was the perfect image for the time. Digital media was just starting to pop and the image showcased a new side of surfing on clunky surf websites the world over. The video was released online a few weeks later and almost broke the old surf movie VHS/DVD model overnight.

But back to Kelly Slater. Always back to Kelly Slater. He was so good, so handsome, so photogenic, so comfortable in the spotlight, so hungry for it that even without the Roxy movement or Laird's übermensch deal, he could have carried surfing out of recession and into the light alone. Shaun Tomson said, "No sportsman in the world anywhere has for so many years been so far ahead of his peers." Yet the massive gap between Kelly and the rest of the field almost undid him. He won five consecutive world titles in the mid-1990s. After his sixth, in 1998, he retired. He was the best in the world. No one was even close. Time for a different challenge, maybe. Time to scale new mountains. Except little did Kelly Slater know his greatest challenge was just hopping on to the world tour.

Andy Irons was born on Kauai to a man who lived, breathed, and ate surf—and also rice, bananas, and avocados. Phil had moved from California to the island in 1970, having caught an early iteration of G-Land surf wanderlust. He lived in a tent on the beach and lived at a subsistence level so he could surf. And surf. And surf, until he got married and had two sons in rapid succession, Andy and Bruce. Divorce soon followed and Phil moved his boys across the street from Pinetrees, one of Kauai's better waves, and the two boys started surfing every single day after school.

Andy was destined for greatness and everyone knew it. Kai "Borg" Garcia, one of the toughest locals around, told me, "I remember watching him as a little kid surfing Pinetrees. You could always see that he had it. Fuckin' hood-rat ripper. Surfing was different for him. Wasn't mechanical. Fuckin' Picasso in the water. Einstein. He looked at the ocean different."

He looked at the ocean different and he also looked different. Most excellent surfers are short little things, built with a low center of gravity for balance. Of course there are exceptions, like Laird Hamilton, but generally surfers are shorter, cuter things.

Andy Irons was not short. And he was not cute. He was proper handsome. As handsome as Kelly, even, but in a more menacing way. Eyes that burned. An aggressive kink in his movement. The kind of energy that is looking for a fight. He also had hair, and good hair. The sort of hair bequeathed to those who trade in normalcy for a life of salt water. All manner of chestnut, hazelnut, with streaks of blonde. And a jaw that made both Laird Hamilton and Hercules burn with jealousy.

He did well in the junior surf events then smashed a talented field at Pipeline as an eighteen-year-old, and then he jumped on the world tour, where he struggled for a few years before starting to put it together for a sixteenth-place finish in 2000 and a tenth-place finish in 2001.

Kelly Slater must have smelled a proper challenge and jumped back on tour himself in 2002, ready to send the kid with a better jaw and better hair packing. Except in 2002, Andy Irons smashed Kelly Slater and smashed him properly. Andy won the trophy. Kelly ended up ninth.

And the fire had been lit. Andy Irons and Kelly Slater battled each other, tooth and nail, for the next five years and it was, officially, the most exciting five-year stretch in competitive surfing's history. Andy won in 2003 with Kelly Slater getting second. Andy won again in 2004 with Kelly falling just short. Three titles in a row. Bam. The two men hated each other, which gave the rivalry a feeling of genuine importance. Like it really mattered. C. J. Hobgood, a wonderful boy from Florida, told me, "Andy was the first person who came along that hated Slater. He hated everything about him, and I know hate is a strong word, but he really hated Kelly." Hate is a strong word, which is exactly what made this rivalry so delicious.

Andy Irons put his imprint on Hawaiian in the same way that Duke Kahanamoku, Eddie Aikau, and Sunny Garcia had. He put his imprint on surf in the same way as Mikey Dora. He put his imprint on the movable surf party like Michael Tomson. It was a great time to be a fan and everyone had a favorite. Either Kelly Slater and his good looks and his good, clean living, which included eating chia seeds, or Andy Irons and his good looks and his rage and his cocaine. So much cocaine. His consumption was a legendary open secret within the surf industry, of which I had just become a card-carrying surf journalist member. Straight from Hezbollah's frying pan into Billabong's trash fire!

Andy was one of the first surfers I was tasked to interview after my "surfing in radical Islamic countries" stories lost their steam. I was part of the bad thing happening in surfing, the curse words and the naughty vibes so clearly Team Andy and not Team Kelly. And I remember getting emailed his cell phone number and just staring at the digits like I was part of some elected mystical few. That I possessed Andy Irons's cell phone number—that was better than having access to Osama bin Laden himself.

I dialed nervously; Andy answered, his voice bouncy and pointed. I asked specifically about his rivalry with Kelly, asking if he would give me some ammo to really drive it up. He half laughed and said, "No, you guys are sure good at that. That's what you guys want…" If he wasn't going to ratchet up his own rivalry, I asked him to start others. He half laughed again and said, "Definitely, you know Jordy and Dane—or it could be getting younger and younger. Little Kolohe Andino mixing it up with some other grom. Or some creepy older molester driving around in a van missing hubcaps looking for kids."

"Kiddie porn?" I asked. "Should there be a kiddie porn rivalry?"

"Yeah, definitely. That's going to be rad," he said, half laughing. Then, "Nah, just kidding. Take this all out of the interview. That's not the direction I wanna be going."

Obviously. But he was fun to talk with. Almost easy.

I saw him from time to time at surf industry parties, loud, brash, wild-eyed. He was the center of any scene he was in since Kelly Slater didn't party and since those who did party loved him precisely because he was one of them, an unmistakable halo of cocaine emanating outward. Glowing. Bathing all in the effortless crescendo of good times and instant (if not secretly greedy) friends.

The surf industry had never been worth more money. The 1980s version of surf chic was dwarfed by Quiksilver and Billabong as the two scooped up investor capital, went public, then went on buying sprees, purchasing smaller surf brands, golf brands, ski brands for small fortunes. Both grew to well over billion-dollar valuations and in typical surf fashion adamantly refused to see the wild growth as cyclical. Of course there was no end in sight. The future only held more good times, more instant (if not secretly holding) friends, and the fattest contracts. Even the worst professional surfer was clearing a million dollars a year through various sponsorships in the heady aughts. Beach rats with more money than they had ever dreamed with nothing to do other than surf, surf, surf, and party in an industry run by slightly older surfers who had figured out how to monetize a lifestyle and still couldn't believe their luck.

And cocaine. Obviously. The surfers' choice since the beginning of time. Since Peru circa 3000 BC. Since G-Land in the 1970s. Since Gotcha's hot eighties nights. Cocaine without end. I couldn't believe the bathroom lines when I first dropped from the Middle East to the surf industry. "Why doesn't everyone just go piss in the parking lot?" I asked a new filmmaker friend.

He just laughed at me.

I suppose, though, that the scene had shifted in tone from Gotcha's hot eighties nights with the companies turning public and with their new consumer being a Midwestern mom buying her son some board shorts from a mall. She didn't know anything about surfing's greatest love affair, and if she did, she sure as hell wouldn't be allowing junior to wear cocaine short pants.

But it was there. It was everywhere. Everywhere and nowhere. A wonderful surf journalist friend told me a story about going to interview a famous professional surfer in his hotel room. When he knocked on the door, he heard a thump as if someone had fallen down, then a scramble; then the professional surfer answered the door with cocaine covering his entire face. "Fuck," he said, "the mosquitos are really bad here," trying to pass off his cocaine makeup as bug spray.

Another told me about stumbling upon three professional surfers having cocaine races where they lined rails of equal size on a coffee table and raced to the finish twenty minutes before one of them paddled out for his heat.

Another told me of going to interview a professional surfer who pointed out a mound of cocaine behind the television and said, "Let's do that instead."

I walked into a room on the North Shore, once, to interview a professional surfer and there was a giant table in the room so dusted with cocaine, like bleached flour, it might have been assumed that the boys were involved in a serious baking competition—except surfers don't do that kind of baking.

I once had to take a professional surfer to the bank and then to his coke dealer before he agreed to talk with me.

But these sorts of stories never went in magazines or movies or on the brand-new Internet. They stayed whispered from one person to another as surfing wrenched itself into a more and more conservative outward-facing position. Taking more and more money from Midwestern mom.

The 2000s were a great time to be a semi-closeted cocaine-loving surfer, but the outside culture had turned sharply away from South America's miracle and were again embracing a man-made 1940s ideal.

Narconon, Scientology's substance abuse treatment and addiction center, reports that 5.7 million people were regular cocaine users in the United States in 1985. That number had dropped to a slight 1.2 million by 2000 with at least one-fifth of those being crack users. The United Nations' Office of Drugs and Crime, maybe a more reliable source than L. Ron Hubbard, noted in their 2000 report on Global Illicit Drug Trends that "cocaine is still the second most widely consumed drug in the USA after cannabis but prevalence in the USA has declined, notably among casual users. According to the Household Survey data, it fell by more than 60 percent since 1985 until the year 2000."

That is a massive drop by either Scientology's estimations or the UN's. The last time cocaine consumption fell so precipitously was because Adolf Hitler had introduced cheap and effective laboratory-produced amphetamines. This time, or so the social scientists say, was due advances in the fun properties of prescription pain pills and Ecstasy.

Methylenedioxymethamphetamine, better known as MDMA and the best part of Ecstasy, had first been synthesized by a German chemist in 1912 with the hope that it could stop abnormal bleeding. It did not work very well and sat on the shelf until an American chemist named Alexander Shulgin became interested in the drug's psychoactive effect. Shulgin was a legend in the world of psychedelics, and even though he was a proper scientist, he was also a massive fucking hippie with a flowing white beard and penchant for elevated ideals and shit. Plus he was born in Berkley, California, so it only made sense that he kicked his findings over to a therapist friend who decided it would be good to give to lovers who were inhibited.

One thing led to another, and by the early 2000s, ravers were pairing warehouses filled with synthwave, balloons, animal costumes, and a heavy downbeat with Ecstasy and a fantastic time. Man had once again shaken a lab-coated fist at God and sent cocaine into a tailspin.

I knew a few surfers during the early 2000s who bit on the MDMA craze, but they were oddballs. Outliers. There was something about the drug's specific attachment to dance music and costumes that turn most surfers off. I think, also, the effect lasts too long with the up coming too gradually and the down also happening too gradually. Surfing is a spike of endorphins. It is seeing a wave stack up on the horizon, paddling like a madman, popping to feet, rushing and then forgetting. Again, the cocaine high mirrors the surf high. The initial quick hit, the quicker dissipation, the lack of memory. The more, more, more. Cocaine. It's got what the surfer needs.

A cocaine-addled professional big-wave surfer bumps into me at the Red Bull premiere, spilling my drink on my Saint Laurent fake Vans, snapping me back into the present day. He apologizes while giggling before pushing off into the crowd that feels increasingly bored. Or maybe boring. And his giggling feels completely unnecessary. I want to scream after him, "Come on. I'm here, aren't I? What more do you need from me? I've given everything. I've given fucking everything, unlike that damned William Finnegan who got to drop into this world, write the best surf book ever in *Barbarian Days*, win a Pulitzer, then drop back out to his real job covering real things at *The New Yorker*." But I don't.

I think about going to the bar and getting another drink, but the line stretches farther back than it should and so I am stuck. Drinkless and thinking about my life and cocaine. A bad combination. That fucking cocaine-addled professional big-wave surfer. The way my heart pounded when I first dialed Andy Irons's cell phone number more than a decade ago now is such a distant memory. Such an almost evaporated sensation. I won't be able to recall it at all soon. Not even a little taste. It'll be gone forever. I realized very early on in my new, mistaken surf journalism career, that it was impossible to be both a fan and a writer. Maybe even weeks after interviewing my first surfer or going to my first surf contest. Maybe even after interviewing Andy Irons. The surf journalist and the professional surfer are two distinct entities often acting at odds against one another.

My clearest and maybe final revulsion with the surf journalist fan was when Mick Fanning called me a "fucking Jew." The man who introduced us was a respected surf journalist. He had written multiple books on professional surfers, had edited the finest Australian magazines, and even started his own blog. He was a name in the tiny world of surf journalism. He saw me early on at the world title party and we got into a conversation about surf writing and maybe even writing in general. He was excited to introduce me to Mick Fanning, and then when Mick Fanning unloaded on me because of rude things I had written about him in the past, the respected surf journalist just stood there with the saddest look on his face underneath a Micktory! hat and above a Micktory! T-shirt. That's right. The respected surf journalist was decked out from head to toe in Mick Fanning world title swag and it was one of the worst looks I had ever seen. Proximity to subject is the kiss of death for fun writing, and at the end of the day that's all I want to do, or at least that's what I've recognized as my only capability.

And I really do need another drink to stop the endless prattle in my head. Another drink or just leave this bullshit behind both like right now, and for, like, ever. There is no way I'm leaving forever. Fun writing exists in one place and one place only anymore. Maybe.

15

The Crossing of the
Return Threshold!

I am home and hungover since I must have gotten in line for another drink at the Red Bull big-wave surf premiere. Either that or someone handed me another drink and maybe some bullshit fake whiskey thing or something, since my head is pounding. *Boom. Boom. Boom.*

But a hangover as the father of a sweet little princess is not an option. Not even a possibility. And she is shaking me in the bed saying, "Papa! Papa! I want pancakes!" And my stomach is churning and my head is pounding but my soul now has an arrow through it and so I stagger up to a sitting position, eyes red and angry, and say, "Yeah, baby girl. With chocolate chips or blueberries?" Vomit almost follows the words "chocolate chips" out of my mouth.

She says, "Chocolate chips!" And I wonder if this is why Andy Irons fucking died. Because there is no way he would have been able to handle his lifestyle, the only lifestyle he had ever known, *and* chocolate chip pancakes. His wife was eight months pregnant with their first and only child before he died alone in a Dallas, Texas, airport hotel room from cocaine and other shit but mostly cocaine.

Love. It is a damned curse. It makes the most sensible people on earth mad. It makes the straight places crooked. It is an absurd son of a bitch that makes Romeo take a poison pill and makes Juliet stab herself in the heart. That makes the Son of God come down from heaven and die on a cross, a torturous death, for a rabble mass of unworthy humanity. Love. Son of a bitch.

And because of love, I stagger to the kitchen and toss a hunk of organic butter onto a skillet and start mixing unpasteurized goat milk with gluten-free pancake mix, and if that's not a recipe for hangover hell, then you have never had a proper hangover.

Fucking bullshit fake whiskey.

Fucking love.

And fucking Andy Irons. His demise rocked the surf industry like no other maybe ever. Oh, there have been plenty of drowning deaths in the past decade. Deaths carried out by the angry vicious will of an angry vicious sea. Eddie Aikau is one of the first and most famous ones. He was a legendary North Shore surfer, an icon in the 1970s and, quite basically, put Waimea Bay on the map. The same one the Beach Boys falsettoed about. "All over La Jolla and Waimea Bay, everybody's gone surfing, surfing USA…" The same one that hosts one of the most famous events in all of surfing: "The Quiksilver in Memory of Eddie Aikau," with its towering waves and feats of super humanity.

Eddie was on the maiden voyage of the Hokule'a, a Hawaiian sailing vessel that replicated those early boats that ancient Hawaiians and Tahitians confounded navigational science with. The crew was going to reenact the ocean crossing between islands and set out from Honolulu on March 17, 1978. Five hours out to sea, the hull sprung a leak and Aikau hopped on a surfboard to paddle to Lanai, the nearest island. A few hours after that the boat was rescued by the Coast Guard.

Eddie Aikau's body was never found.

Dickie Cross had drowned while trying to paddle from Sunset to Waimea when the surf unexpectedly jumped in 1943. Any surfer who has been out in Hawaii when the swell starts to suddenly grow feels Dickie Cross's terror in his own heart. Todd Chesser drowned at

Outer Alligator's on the North Shore. Tahitian standout Malik Joyeux drowned at Pipeline. Sion Milosky from Kauai drowned at Maverick's in Northern California eight years after North Shore standout Mark Foo did the same.

The list goes on and on and on and has always been infused with nobility. Mark Foo always recognized the possibility that his passion could very well lead to his death and once told a television news interviewer, "It would be a glamorous way to go, a great way to go; I mean, that's how I'd like to go out." And that's how he did go out. Drowned with his surfboard leash caught around one of Maverick's rocks while engaged to be married. A painful blow.

Tragic but honorable, or at least honorable to the pterygium-eyed surfer. The surfer who has happily and knowingly traded their eyes for a sensation. But fucking Andy Irons, a hero, a legend, a party machine, an epically talented surfer, a handsome son of a bitch, died alone in a Dallas, Texas, airport hotel room at thirty-two years old on his way home after pulling out of a surf contest in Puerto Rico because he said he was "sick."

Everyone in the surf industry—every brand manager, professional surfer, surf journalist, Association of Surfing Professionals employee—knew that Andy Irons either had too much or hadn't had enough. That he was either hungover from a massive Portuguese bender or withdrawing from the lack of a massive Portuguese bender. Any who claim ignorance, who really thought he was "sick," are either lying or so naive as to be a danger to themselves and others. The surf world knew Andy Irons.

The news started trickling out immediately. I was in Zurich, Switzerland, when I heard and felt a profound sadness mixed with rage. Usually death doesn't bother me. I have the Christian bonus of believing that heaven is real, but his felt like a nasty and unnecessary shot. It felt like the oxygen had been let out of the room, and all this, all that we do, is worthless and bad and a profound waste of time. It was too early, too absurd—too crass, even.

Billabong, his primary sponsor, released a short statement:

The world of surfing mourns an incredibly sad loss today with the news that Hawaii's Andy Irons has died. Andy was a beloved husband, and a true champion. Irons, 32, withdrew from a professional surfing event in Puerto Rico last weekend due to illness and passed away during a layover en route to his home in Kauai, Hawaii. He had reportedly been battling with dengue fever, a viral disease. At this time the family thanks his friends and fans for their support, and asks that the community respect its privacy. The family also asks to not be contacted so their focus can remain on one another during this time of profound loss.

Dengue Fever.

Only very poor people living in the Third World die from Dengue Fever. Not professional surfing millionaires flying from Portugal to Puerto Rico to Dallas. Something was clearly not right, something was not being shared, but the only surf journalist to chase the truth was a *Surfer* magazine editor named Brad Melekian, and in chasing it he basically ended his surf journalism career.

None of the magazines or media would touch the story because they wouldn't want to offend a key advertiser. The surf industry's wild growth had started to slow but the apocalypse hadn't begun yet and print hadn't died yet. These were still the salad years, the brands held the purse strings, and any outlet or person who stepped out of line would be cut off.

So Brad went outside the surf industry, to Santa Fe-based *Outside Magazine*, and penned one of the more impressive pieces of surf reportage. His story, "Last Drop," detailed never-before-revealed details of Andy's struggle with booze, pills, and cocaine. He interviewed people who were in Indonesia eleven years earlier when Andy flatlined after drinking quarts of Jack Daniel's and taking who knows what. He interviewed ex-magazine editors about how in the pocket of the brands surf media is. He interviewed ex-employees of Andy's other sponsors, who said that the company he worked for was certainly aware of their star's drug problem. He revealed that Andy Irons had been to rehab more than once and had wanted to come clean to the surf media about his struggles, but his plan was allegedly scuttled by Billabong because the brand allegedly didn't want the bad press.

Melekian then went about chronologically putting Andy Irons' last few days together, a mission I'm certain even Sherlock Holmes would have failed. Surfers are, remember, viciously shallow and used to lying through their teeth. Obfuscating. Throwing smoke to hide waves, plans, anything from each other and the world. It is a deadly combination when searching for truth. I'm certain Sherlock Holmes would have given up after three days, banging his head against a wall, screaming, "It's NOT elementary, dear Watson! Who are these monsters?"

Apparently Irons didn't show up for his heat in Puerto Rico, complained he was sick, and asked for a doctor but fled when he thought he might have to submit a blood test and demanded to go home. A Billabong representative claimed he was on an IV for two days in Miami, which was not true, and other reports suggested that he was kept off his flight from Dallas, heading to Honolulu, because he was too ill, which was also not true.

Melekian finished off his story with a touching quote from Andy where he said, "Surfing is the closest thing you can feel by being kissed by God." It came out before the toxicology report was released, and the surf world, the cloistered little surf world, came after him with pitchforks and torches.

And I was leading that viciously shallow charge. Waving my pitchfork with an ugly, but maybe also gleeful, sneer smeared across my face. I was writing for *Surfing Magazine* at the time, read Melekian's piece, and smashed out an Andy Irons eulogy glorifying his partying, his wild side, and the surf world closing ranks and keeping damned magazines from Santa Fe outside. I spewed:

And so the deliciousness, the salaciousness, of a young and handsome and wild surfer being possibly felled by wrong, dangerous drugs and all the tawdry details being kept quiet by the family is almost too much. The outside world wants it all, the judgment, the smugness, and mask their lust for dirt beneath cloaks of honest concern and the demand for journalistic integrity. And many who surf will even agree.

And they can continue to go to hell.

His death is a tragedy of epic proportions but Andy Irons lived his life to epic proportions. He was bigger than virtually everything. And the chemical compounds floating in black and white on a toxicology report, whenever it is released, change nothing. Absolutely nothing. For floating alone, divorced from the endless complexities of his life, they are no better than statistics. Worse than damned lies.

What an asshole. What a total dick. What an utterly hypocritical prick.

My point, if I can dig through the weeds clogging the dirt-filled hole where my memories are supposed to go, was that it didn't matter that Andy Irons died of a drug overdose. Surfing was fun, it was good, it was right because it wasn't trying to be a sport or a religion or anything other than what it was: unadulterated fun. Once drug testing and all that sort of stuff came in, then surfing would be a sport. I already played football in seventh and eighth grade and didn't need to do that again. I was the skinniest thing ever born and got smashed so often and so severely that my two-season football career is probably responsible for the dirt-filled hole. That or navigating by smartphone.

I already went to church; I didn't need any more moralizing in the water. If surfers wanted to find God, to kiss Him as it were, they could go to church, too. So I popped off telling everyone, all the non-endemic media, to go to hell. This surfing was filled with cocaine and that's the way we liked it. Or at least the way I liked it.

I knew the toxicology report would come back with cocaine and whatever else and that would be that. That surfing's love story killed Andy Irons. I didn't want him to be a cautionary tale. All surfers are already a cautionary tale. Surf history is a cautionary tale. Making Andy Irons a trite "what not to do" was too much. The mamas of the world already knew not to let their babies grow up to be surfers. Michael Tomson warned them off years ago. If you don't surf, don't start! But maybe he should be. Maybe he should be a giant DON'T DO DRUGS poster. Either way, dealing honestly with the truth internally was going to be refreshing.

And then the Irons family delayed it and delayed it again. I remember talking to his manager at the time and saying, "Just release it already. Who cares? Everyone already knows that he partied. Almost everyone has partied with him." His manager told me, "I think you'll be surprised. I don't think the cause of death is what you think it is."

And then it came out listing "heart attack" as the primary factor due to a hardening of the arteries from an undiagnosed condition with a secondary cause of "acute mixed drug ingestion"—particularly methadone, and of course cocaine. The family had hired its own pathologist to further throw smoke. Dr. Vincent Di Maio wrote that it was his professional opinion Andy died of a heart attack due to hardening of the arteries and that there were no other contributing factors to his death.

The Association of Surfing Professionals backed away from any hint that Irons died of a drug overdose and released a statement celebrating his "unbridled passion." His family released a statement that read, "Traveling while sick and suffering from an undiagnosed heart condition was more than even Andy could overcome." The most trafficked website in all of surf, *Surfline*, who regularly gets angry with me, sent out a tweet reading, "Andy Irons died of sudden cardiac arrest due to a blocked artery. His heart was full of passion for life & surfing."

And I thought, "Bull-fucking-shit."

The thing stank to high heaven. Worse than anything, for me, was not recognizing the love story, even if it is the sickest of all, and it seemed like heresy. It seemed rude and awful and unnecessary. I had witnessed Andy Irons going completely mad. Anyone and everyone connected to the surf industry in those years had. To claim "hardening of the arteries" just seemed blasphemous. Andy Irons wasn't a geriatric. He wasn't an old man suffering from atherosclerosis. His heart wasn't full of passion for "life & surfing." It was full of methadone, Ambian, Xanax, and cocaine, and I can't imagine he would want to be remembered as anything other than what he was. In my brief conversations with him, it was abundantly clear that he valued truth, or at least honesty.

When someone got in his ear, he might back down, but fuck.

Andy Irons knew.

I suppose with many drug-related deaths there is always some primary factor that causes the actual death itself. Elvis Presley died of atherosclerosis, which lead to a heart attack and a smashed head. Dr. Finkle, a consultant in the Presley case, claimed in a 1977 *Salt Lake City Tribune* interview that, "We have not detected any drug in Elvis that doesn't have a medical rationale to it—only agents prescribed for perfectly normal, rational medical reasons." As the years passed, though, and journalists, writers, and doctors dug into the evidence, it became apparent that Elvis had a massive prescription painkiller problem. Whitney Houston's cause of death was officially drowning with a secondary cause of atherosclerotic heart disease. Again, she had cocaine and Xanax in her system. But again, neither were the direct cause of death.

Andy Irons, Elvis Presley, and Whitney Houston. The American Heart Association's leading figures in reminding citizens that a balanced diet, exercise, and regular checkups are an essential part to a long and healthy life. Is that the takeaway here?

Melekian doubled down a few weeks after the autopsy was released, penning a second piece for *Outside*, even better than the first, titled "Crashing Down," skewering the surf industry's twisting of the truth, if not outright lies. Its "wall of silence." He was called into Billabong's Irvine office by the then CEO, a South African named Paul Naude who is now the CEO of surf brand Vissla and the then VP of marketing, a South African named Graham Stapelberg, who was once slapped by Eddie Rothman. He was supposed to "explain himself" for his first story.

Naude and Stapelberg answered some questions too in order to "set the record straight," about Andy's drug use, his trips to rehab, how both the brand and the surf community tried to help him, how Billabong had fined him for his drug use. But there was also a heavy veneer of passive-aggression. Naude told Melekian that "(Andy's toxicology) results represented an 'inconvenient truth' for journalists like (him)." That surf journalists were hoping it was a drug overdose because it was tawdry, I suppose. Salacious.

The two also denied using the brand's leverage to try and silence the surf media by calling it "typical speculation." Melekian wrote that Paul Naude contended that Andy Irons decided not to come clean to the surf media all by himself. "We said to him, 'It's a private matter at this stage. If you choose to keep it private, that's your decision. If you choose to go public because you think it'll make you feel better, then go public.'"

Even in a total spin, it reads funny and I have no idea what Naude and Stapelberg consider, or considered, "a private matter," but Andy Irons' love of the party was certainly not unknown. Multiple surf journalists had received a heads-up that Andy was finally going to come clean before he disappeared. Not one of them wondered what he was going to come clean about.

Melekian wrapped his piece by introducing a very gorgeous surf journalist from Oregon by way of Lebanon. "Most surf writers have closed ranks and argued that how Irons died is irrelevant; we should be focusing on how he lived," he wrote. "But that's not exactly true. Trivializing his problems, as *Surfing* contributing writer Chas Smith did when he wrote in an online essay that people who want to know the truth 'can continue to go to hell,' is an attempt both to fabricate his legacy and to absolve the people around him of any responsibility. Smith, in his essay, also made what is perhaps the most telling point about the saga, writing himself into the Irons clan as he went: 'The family kept, and keeps, his failures behind a closed door precisely because we are a family.'"

Oops. What an asshole. What a dick. What a prick. Trivializing cocaine abuse and writing myself into a story I'm not a real part of. I fought for my overall premise for months, years even. Surfing's failures belong to surfing, to the surf industry, because *we* know what the truth is. Right? We know and can bounce different opinions about how to handle that truth off each other. Right?

I was not right, and it was the utter self-deception in the Andy Irons story that gutted me. I thought, "Yeah, he did tons of cocaine and tons of whatever else and his death was beyond sad and totally senseless but, at the end, that's what surfing is, too. It is beautiful because it is senseless. It is gorgeous because it doesn't have to be anything it is not." I wasn't prepared to be fed a line about heart attacks and hardening of the arteries. An inconvenient bending of the truth is what it was, or at least a willful misreading of what was going on every day in the surf industry. About the entire trajectory from 3000 BC until this very moment. Worst of all, that is the story that keeps getting driven out internally.

Poor Andy Irons and his hard arteries and his untreated bipolar condition. I don't doubt he had both those, but he also just liked drugs too much and I know, I *know*, that I should feel more than this. Partly responsible for witnessing a corner of the madness and not doing much about it. And in many ways I do. But maybe it's just in a tabloid clickbait sort of way. Maybe in a "Breaking: Surfer dead of overdose!" way.

I don't fucking know.

And Brad Melekian? He disappeared from surf journalism after the last *Outside* story hit shelves. I had heard whispers that he was supposed to write the Andy Irons book but then the Irons family refused to grant any interviews, leaving him high and dry and headed back into academia and real, meaningful work.

But I stayed behind, accidentally—and apparently forever. A surf journalist. Cursed. A still hungover father making gluten-free goat milk pancakes and choking back vomit.

The Andy Irons thing made me realize how duplicitous the surf industry is to its own damned conservative detriment. So stiff. So Orange County scrubbed. So tight. So paranoid. That it would happily void the parts that made it unique in order to serve some artificial nothing.

I vowed if anything like him ever happened again, I would chase the motherfucker. I would gnash and grind and pull and tug until surfing's greatest love was let out of the closet and into the light even if the light were fluorescent and exposed so many blemishes. I would set cocaine and surfing free. I would bring the world's oldest love story to the masses and I would be the hero and hopefully end up someplace meaningful like academia. Or…Just kidding. I am not nearly intelligent enough for academia nor talented enough for anything else. I will be a surf journalist until I die. A surf journalist at forty, at fifty, at sixty. I will never leave, but I'll drag surfing, kicking and screaming, back into the light.

16

World Dancer!

The weeks roll by and then the months. I bounce back and forth between chasing cocaine and wondering if somehow my journey is fatally flawed. Kicking at the surf industry's goads while wondering if all the brand managers, team managers, executive vice presidents, surf journalists, and professional surfers are right to keep their love hidden behind a big black burqa. I post COCAINE + SURFING: A LOVE STORY! on *BeachGrit* and the stories start trickling in, then gushing. About one professional surfer getting lost for ten days in Brazil while on a cocaine bender. About late nights and waking up next to unfortunate people. About dancing and conversations and the foolish things done in pursuit of more cocaine but only mildly foolish.

Most of them, to be frank, are dull. Almost all of them are, in fact, and I wonder if there is a problem with cocaine itself. If somehow the ancient powder transforms its supplicants into simpletons. As ugly as methamphetamine is, I've heard many hilarious stories of people getting artistic or at least very weird while high. I had a lawyer once who smoked meth then decided he was going to create a work of art by cutting a plate-glass window in half on a table saw. It did not end well, but it's still funny.

There are good psychedelic LSD, mushroom, etc. stories, too. Surfing all night under a full moon while monsters chase. Or putting a surfboard in a bathtub and trying to get barreled under the spout. Or surfing naked over a very shallow reef while singing "Auld Lang Syne."

But cocaine stories generally start and end in one place: the bathroom. A pack of sweaty men standing around a toilet jabbering to each other all night. A pack of sweaty women dancing to the worst music with mascara-smeared eyes.

As my best Australian pal and biz partner says, "Women to whores, men to bores."

I even found an eight ball of cocaine on the street—while walking my adorable daughter's Chihuahua—tucked into the spine of an old, discarded *Surfing Magazine*, of all ironic things. God was giving me everything I needed to celebrate the love story properly. I ran home, stuck my key into the bag, grabbed my board, and went for a surf. What better way to consummate? The water seemed colder, the sun extra bright. I couldn't stop clenching my jaw. I got into a very serious conversation with another surfer bobbing in the water about the merits of carbon-wrapped surfboard rails versus traditional wooden stringer construction. When I got home, I had a migraine.

It was not very exceptional, though still kind of amusing.

And then, one winter's day, almost five years after Andy Irons died near Dallas in an airport hotel room, it happened again. I was heading down to check the surf on a warm winter's day, going to possibly work on my wetsuit neck tan line, when the text popped into my phone from a fellow surf journalist.

"Did you hear?"

I texted back, "No."

And then a story rushed through that I knew was cocaine plus surfing. It featured a horrible accident. A strange, initial, incomprehensible explanation pushed out to the surf media. A completely weird twist of logic from a surf brand. Classic love story denial, and I was on the case. This was my moment.

Except this time the surfer did not die. A blessed thing, but it also meant no autopsy, no toxicology, no way to get at the truth without firing on all surf journalist cylinders. I started making calls. Pushing.

Prodding. Digging. Leveraging any and all relationships I had in a quest for bright truth. Trying to force the closet door open with all my might.

More weeks passed.

Then more months.

And the story began to develop which felt like a major cover-up. Whispers about how mad the surfer had been going in the few months prior to the accident. Friends of friends of friends who had warned him to slow down. There was surprise, even in the most coke-addled little corner, over how much he was consuming. Then rumors began to pop up in online message boards and around social media. The truth was right there, right at my fingertips, and this was my chance to come correct. This was my real chance to break it all free.

But I couldn't, no matter how much I tried, no matter what I promised, get anyone who had been in the world's bathroom stalls with the injured surfer to go on the record. Some were afraid of his main sponsor brand's wrath. Some didn't think it was their place to crack it open. Some accused me of wanting to destroy the young man's life.

"Destroy his life?" I thought. "No way! I'm giving him his life back. He won't have to carry some absurd, clearly dubious story regarding how his injury happened. He'll be free!"

But was I setting out to destroy his life? His sponsors certainly knew the truth, right? What would they care if it came out because no Midwestern moms are buying board shorts for junior anymore? All the mall stores have gone bankrupt and closed. The only people paying attention to surf, the only people buying anything surf-related, are surfers themselves. And surfers feel the love story if they don't know it outright, right? Surfers deserve to know the truth.

But this wasn't Watergate. This wasn't Iran-Contra. Lives were not being severely altered by a probable cocaine accident being sold to the public as something else. The heavy wet blanket of conservative surf industry silence. The cold hands that strangle the life out of surfing itself was what I wanted to rip away, but was I the only one who cared?

Am I the only one who cares?

I emailed a proper journalist who worked for a proper paper and had written a story on the incident that was cut by his editor because there was no smoking gun. No one willing to go on the record for him, either. I was threatened with vague legal action by a groupie.

I kept smashing out the love story, feeling its swell, feeling myself transform from surf journalist to narc to prophet to hypocrite to gutter writer. I kept bashing my head against the outside limit of my talent, trying to get to the bottom of the new cover-up even while my stomach revolted at what I was doing. At the narrative that I was pushing out. That cocaine plus surfing is not a love story. It is a tragedy. A fucking tragedy, and worse still, it is boring.

And now, in my low moment of despair, I am emailing Brad Melekian because I need to know how he did it. Even though I led a pitchforked mob against him. Even though I called him many names, maybe worst of all "kook." Maybe even "fucking kook from Santa Fe," even though I know he lives somewhere in Southern California. I need to know how he broke through and why he broke out.

He somehow responds and we exchange a few emails and he agrees to meet. Not only does he live somewhere in Southern California, he lives in Encinitas, California, and now teaches full-time at San Diego State. Basically next door. Part of me can't believe it because calling someone a "kook" is an almost unforgivable offense. At first we decide on coffee even though I try to push a cheap bar, but then my daughter falls asleep so I ask if he can come to my house. He agrees.

He walks through the gate and I am holding a freshly mixed vodka grape-flavored-coconut-water cocktail. He is well built, wearing a tight blue flannel shirt that emphasizes both shoulders and biceps. He has every right to slap me, but his eyes betray him. They are sensitive pools.

We chat for a moment and I apologize for being an asshole. He smiles warmly and accepts, then we move to our once shared career. I ask him what his experience was as a surf journalist. He says, "I guess my experience was that basic procedures of journalism no one knew how to do. Like, fact-checking was a problem. When fact-checkers started calling, people would say, 'Uhhhhh. I only talk to my bro...' stuff like that. I feel like, when Andy died, all of us were out of our depth a little bit. I was used to writing three-thousand-word profiles that might have a little bit of meat to them. Then, with the Andy story, it was all, 'Okay, who is willing to go on the record? Who is willing to say what actually happened?' And that was the interesting thing: I would have really in-depth, one-hundred-percent forthright conversations off the record, and then I'd say, 'Okay, I'm gonna start recording now.' And guys would just go full crickets. Not wanting to talk. Not willing to say anything."

My stomach turns and I ask him, why? What is our fucking problem with the truth? Is it all that dangerous? He sits back while I sip my mixed vodka grape-flavored-coconut-water cocktail and thinks for a minute then says, "Surfing is one of the most arch-conservative subcultures in the world. You talk about being risk averse. These guys are really conservative and they don't know what's going to happen to their careers if they say the wrong thing."

My stomach turns again. Of course I agree with him. The conservative. My enemy. My foil. So why the hell did I lash out against a fellow fighter? I ask him if it hurt and his eyes melt me when he says, "The backlash, I expected, but what I didn't expect..." he pauses and collects himself. "Yeah. I'd get mad. When you were going off, I tried to see the humor in it, but then I was like, ugh. Because more than anything I was sad. There is no way you can look at the whole picture— Lyndie being pregnant, that still punches me in the gut when I think about it. It's just a really sad human story, which is also so predictable. There's a pro surfer that has a drug problem and he's a drug addict and he had a hard time managing that. That to me seemed like a really normal human story. A tragic one, and one that happens every day in really sad ways and that bummed me out. Then for all of us to be fighting each other while that was taking place seemed like it totally missed the point."

My stomach would turn yet again, though still very much enjoying the vodka grape-flavored-coconut-water cocktail. It is such a wonderful surprise. And I ask if he would have continued to be a surf journalist if I wasn't such a dick. His eyes smile this time and he says, "Yeah, I think so, probably. I was already starting to teach, so I was on my way out a little bit, but that was the first thing that put me face-to-face with all of the realities, seeing the bigger players in the surf industry and how they perceived things. You know, a thirty-two-year-old guy died alone in a hotel room in Texas and it didn't seem to change anything for anybody, and that was really dispiriting. And he was a guy that was so beloved by everyone, but the way to show respect was buying one of these Billabong AI Forever hats. Like… fuck. That is the way to deal with the problems that he had? It was difficult for me to respect the industry."

The fucking surf industry. It has taken drugs and placed them square into arch-conservative framework. Cocaine is now the bread and the wine. It is the Eucharist. I ask him what should happen. Should surfing finally clean up? Should it get sober? He leans forward and says, "One thing I think surfing can do is present itself as it is. Like that's fine. If it would just be honest about it. I don't know if there should be drug testing or not, but if we're not going to acknowledge there is a deep connection between surf and the drug culture, like somehow not recognize that because, what, now we have non-endemic sponsors? It doesn't fit."

He is a man after my own heart and I really can't believe I called him a fucking kook from Santa Fe. I really can't believe I chased him away, but maybe I can take a lesson from him. Maybe I can turn my pitchfork into a mantle. And I ask him what the point of all this is. What is the point of surf journalism?

He scratches one of his impressive biceps and says, "When I worked at *Surfer* I would always get told, 'This isn't the *Wall Street Journal*.' And I would be like, 'Okay I get it, we're not the *Wall Street Journal*, but that doesn't mean…'" He stops, searching for words. "Matt Warshaw told me, 'Surf journalism is at its best when it's not moonlighting as surf advocacy.' And that's how I feel. Nobody needs to be told how great it feels to go surfing. But there are some stories that matter. Could a rigid surf journalism be sustained? I don't think so. But the thing that can be done…when people are lying to your face, you don't have to go along with it."

I have a thousand more questions. I need guidance. I need his helping hand, but my little diva wakes up and comes downstairs angry that I wasn't standing by the bed when she woke up holding a tray of salami and grapes. "Who is he?" she asks with a sneer in her voice.

I tell her, "This is Brad Melekian. I was an asshole to him."

She looks at me with a scrunched up face and asks, "What did you do asshole?" She uses "asshole" like an adverb instead of a noun, which is wise beyond years. Like, "Why is he driving asshole?" Or "Papa is being asshole to the neighbors again."

I try to explain and mumble something about surf journalism and the fight against arch-conservatism, but she gets bored and starts playing with her doll that poops magical buttons then goes over to the neighbors' house to do "yoga," which I think includes dressing in princess dresses, putting lipstick on, and screaming that she's a teenager now so everybody needs to shut up.

Brad leaves after a few moments and I stumble upstairs still unclear, uncertain, trying to figure out a way forward. Trying to figure out how to shine the light. And I still don't know, so I sit at my computer and email Nick Carroll, the older brother of the great helmet-wearing Tom Carroll. A man who would be president of the surf journalist union if such a thing existed. The most famous surf journalist of all.

Nick has been writing surf for longer than I've been alive. He's edited surf magazines, written surf books, catalogued this damned passion for generations. He is a proper surf journalist legend and the most handsome under-five-foot-tall man alive with a rock solid jaw and piercing eyes. I realize, when I think about Nick's jaw, and I think about Grapes the Cat, Fred Hemmings, Mitt Romney, Gavin Newsom, Jeff Hakman, Shaun Tomson, Laird Hamilton, and Andy Irons, and how much of a jaw fetish I have. Strange, maybe, but I don't have time to ponder my kink with male aesthetics because I feel that surfing is finally driving me crazy. Truly mad. So I am emailing Nick Carroll, "What is a surf journalist supposed to do?"

He must sense my desperation because he emails his response before I even have time to mix another vodka grape-flavored-coconut-water cocktail and finish Katy Perry's music video for "Chained to the Rhythm," a truly ghastly pop expression.

"The surf journalist's job has varied over the years," he writes. "Sometimes it has been actual reporting, sometimes (recently) historical anecdote, sometimes memoir, etc. I think for a while it was all about trying to get hold of and write about what seemed like a new way of living that nobody's parents had ever done, you know, the classic baby boomer utopia trip. Trying to explain surfing itself? Every journalist would have a different idea of his or her mission in the field. Increasingly since the 1980s, surf journalism has become about connecting the readership to the surf stars, and increasingly this has been co-opted by the surf industry as part of its marketing effort. In recent times some of that has been broken open again—the reporting instinct keeps resurfacing in odd places, it's hard to keep down.

"What I think the surf journalist is supposed to do? Follow his or her nose. What's interesting to you? Struggle against co-option—this is very hard in a small society like surfing. Even journalists like to get along. Don't report rumors, look for substance. Put events into context, explain as much as you can."

Follow my nose. Struggle against co-option. Don't report rumors. Put events into context. Explain as much as I can. But what of the morality? The covering up of a lie versus the potential destruction of a young man's life? Nick is particularly helpful here because he wrote the book outing his brother Tom, the helmet-wearing clean-cut poster child for hard work and good living. Nobody outside the very inner professional surf world knew that Tom Carroll loved cocaine and methamphetamine. He surfed in a pre-Internet era and didn't live the glamorous public life of Michael Tomson. He could have kept his secrets hidden forever. I email, "Why did Tom come clean in your book? Is there always a time and a place to fess up?"

He emails back, "Well that's a personal decision. In the case of 'TC.' I thought it wasn't so much about confession as explanation, not just what happened but why the fuck it happened. You can confess to your priest; the world requires explanation. Tom had the courage and poise to go with it, not everyone would, then again they might not have a nasty older brother either."

I chuckle. I'm a nasty older brother too. A mean, door-kicking bastard. So was Andy Irons. The nastiest older brother. Stories about how he used to abuse his younger brother, Bruce, are traded like baseball cards in the surf industry. And what about Andy? If the surf industry had let his story out, if surf journalists had chased it and not chased Brad Melekian instead, would he still be alive? I ask and Nick Carroll takes a few minutes this time, allowing me to drink another vodka grape-flavored-coconut-water cocktail and watch Sinéad O'Connor's "Nothing Compares 2 U," Madonna's "Ray of Light," and REM's "Losing my Religion."

"What I think, just from observation, is that Andy's drug abuse had roots well beyond the purview of the surf industry. But the surf culture has been enabling drug abuse for fifty years. It was enabled, nay encouraged, among AI's parents' generation, and it was exalted through the romanticizing of great surfers and their drug habits—Michael Peterson, Hakman, good god, on and on and on—and by the mythmaking around the Brotherhood of Eternal Love and other smuggling and selling networks. Put a booming industry and million-dollar pro surfing salaries on top of that and, well, boom. AI just fell into this matrix of enablement in which his addictions were able to flourish, and he hasn't been the only one—just the most famous.

"It was an appalling thing and I think it laid a kind of curse on anyone who bore any kind of witness to it and did nothing in response. Some of those people are still walking around today under the delusion that either they did all they could for him, or it was all Andy's doing and they had no part in it. Others have made real changes in their lives as a result, to their credit. I think overall, drug use in elite surfing has become less acceptable post-AI but that matrix of secrecy and enablement still exists, weakened, but it's still there."

And the last little pieces of my cock-certainty vanish. The final bits of Shakespearean grandeur. The outermost drips of my amusement.

The love story is just a lie. It is like Donald Trump and Melania Trump née Knavs. Fake. Artificial. I slump in my chair and read the sentence "I think it laid a kind of curse on anyone who bore any kind of witness to it…" again and again.

I knew I was cursed. I knew in the deepest part of my heart that surf journalism was profanity. That I would have been better off hunkering down with Hezbollah. Following them to Syria, even. Andy Irons is no more than a cautionary tale, Michael Tomson an impossible dream, those early surf explorers who glassed cocaine into fins and bought surf companies bad examples, and the Peruvians who first surfed and first felt the magic of coca? They were just pushers. No better than drug dealers who loiter outside of junior high schools, pressing the most vulnerable into lives of servitude.

I ask him one more question about the recent potential cover-up. He writes a beautiful response but all off the record, ending with a poignant thought. "There is a new mantra underpinning the whole secrecy thing in the surf industry: that is, it's all okay, everyone does it at some time, as long as it's not addiction. The idea that a great lie may be in the process of being told by omission, and that it may be part of the same enablement that helped AI blow up so horribly, doesn't seem to penetrate many skulls. Nor the consequences of perpetuating such a lie, which they all should know by now—this isn't the foolhardy eighties or whatever."

And I push away from my computer and stumble down stairs to mix a last, or maybe last, vodka grape-flavored-coconut-water cocktail.

17

Master of Two Worlds!

So it's all over. I'm standing at the zinc kitchen counter that I had insisted upon, aesthetically, even though sea air attaches to zinc and corrodes it almost instantly, looking at the pock marks in a daze. Love story. There is no love story. There is nothing but dullness and tragedy. Tragedy in the dullness and dullness in the tragedy. The foolhardy eighties. That's exactly what I wanted for surfing today. The bold sin. The unhinged parties. The open, even disdainful, mockery of those who were not part of the smallest, hardest, shallowest subculture. The complete and utter lack of care for what the future may bring.

The opposite of conservative. The ostentatious.

And before that, before the eighties rock 'n' rollers, the smuggling surf heroes. Those who set out across the sea, running away from crowds and feeling what they loved most was being co-opted. Those who created their own Shangri-Las where they could surf and surf and surf and smuggle cocaine to pay for more surfing.

And before that the postwar Malibu kids who shucked conformity from their lives and ordered their priorities around one of the most pointless things ever. A thing with no future, no perceivable economic benefit, no political clout. A simple, shallow fun thing that didn't make any real sense.

And before that the Polynesians who would stop crushing each other's bones for a moment and run *en masse* to the ocean to ride waves in total and reckless abandon. All work is reported to have stopped when the waves turned on even if it meant starvation. Ancient Hawaiian culture was rigidly stratified but in the water, when surfing, none of it mattered. Kings, peasants, men and women each enjoyed the pointless together.

And before that the Peruvian fishermen who came in from the day's fish, cheeks full of coca, and had fun for maybe the only time in their ugly, cold, perpetually shrouded-in-cold-mist lives. Because nothing is as fun as riding waves. Nothing is as fun as surfing and God damn those who try desperately to squeeze the life out of it all. Who try and turn it into something it never was and never should be: timid, bourgeois, hidebound. Conservative.

I picture Michael Tomson in his new San Clemente home with his towering achievements and his burning failures having basically been ejected from the surf industry for being too flamboyant. I remember him glowing about Elmore Leonard. "Characters. You've got to have characters. Elmore Leonard kind of characters. Characters that *do* something. The what for is in the characters. The story is in the characters. And they are so *fucking* hip, so *fucking* good it is actually unbelievable."

So fucking hip, so fucking good it is actually unbelievable. Like a South African surfer starting a global fashion empire. Like Mike Boyum discovering G-Land, smuggling cocaine, and meeting some mystical end. Like Jeff Hakman glassing cocaine into his fins and buying Quiksilver. Like Andy Irons who caught the surf world on fire for one brief moment and was just as quickly extinguished. Surf history is littered with fabulous characters. The most fabulous tied inextricably to cocaine.

And I'm staring at the corrosion pocks in my poor zinc and I'm sipping the last of the last vodka grape-flavored-coconut-water cocktail since I'm now out of both grape-flavored coconut water and vodka and it dawns on me, finally. The fabulous characters aren't interesting because of cocaine. Cocaine is interesting because of them. And suddenly I have the urge, for the first time in my life, to write fiction. The surf industry CEO and brand manager, team manager, executive vice president, head of global marketing covering up the latest cocaine overindulgence/accident can all go to hell.

I'll create a new cast of characters from my imagination. Characters that spark the imagination and fire the heart. Characters that are truly representative of who we are.

I run back upstairs, stumbling again, throw my computer's lid open and open up a new document. The computer screen is there, blank, but I feel inspired. I am going to be a surf novelist. I am going to make literary surf art.

After an hour of watching more music videos and playing a game of *Grand Theft Auto* on my broken phone while realizing there is no way my imagination could ever conjure a Michael Tomson, an email pops up on my screen from my best Australian pal and biz partner. It reads, "The WSL is using a giant blow-up Tyrannosaurus rex with a man inside to try and win a Webby! It's on Facebook Live!"

I Google "Webby" and see it is like the Academy Awards of the Internet. Or maybe the Golden Globes. I log onto Facebook and watch a strange insecure boy sitting in a chair on Santa Monica's beach with a sign begging for people to vote the World Surf League's website over the NFL and professional wrestling. The Tyrannosaurus is called "Shredosaurus." The insecure boy is saying, "Come on. Vote for us. We're better than... what's the NFL? Oh. The football where men hit each other and stuff. We're sick! We're way better than that. Vote and Shredosaurus paddles out and gets some bombs!"

I hurry over to *BeachGrit* to post "Barney: The WSL wants a Webby!" and the words flow fast and furiously. I am inspired. I am a machine. I am a surf journalist. It takes me exactly six minutes to write it up, find a picture, and post the story. I sit back, read, and chuckle at my own work. It is good and I deserve a reward so I head back downstairs for another cocktail before realizing that I finished everything. All the grape-flavored coconut water. All the vodka.

Damn it.

I fish in the fridge and find an old Stella Artois stuck in the back corner. I don't drink beer, on principal, but beggars can't be choosers so pull it out and decide to drink it at the beach.

The road is mostly empty as I saunter down the hill and the sunset is straight from God's brush, all manner of orange, pink, red, fire, passion, glory. I sit on a wooden bench that overlooks my favorite wave on earth. It is breaking but not very good. A handful of older men on soft-top longboards are making assholes of themselves but at least it's something to watch.

A dolphin jumps out of the water. An airplane flies one more lonely circle towing a sign that reads, CHEETAH'S GENTLEMAN'S CLUB. A mom and dad finish packing up their beach wagon while their two children throw sand in each other's faces.

And then my phone buzzes in my pocket. I fish it out, accidentally bringing the Stella with it, but thankfully it lands on the bench and doesn't hit the ground. Drinking dirt would be gross. I look and see a Facebook message from my foil Ian Cairns, the father of professional surfing, the one-time Bronzed Aussie, my foil who dislikes actively provoking riots and gutter writing. We had just gotten into it again, this time over standup paddleboards or SUPs. They are an absolute abomination in my opinion. He likes them. I wrote a story declaring standup paddlers should all die. He posted on Facebook that he loves standup paddling if only because it differentiates him from the gutter writer. His fans hammered me with all manner of "go to hell" and "shut up, kook."

I enjoy the vitriolic back-and-forth, but nobody else ever does. Nobody apparently except Ian Cairns. His note reads, "G'Day mate, Nice to joust. It's a fine Aussie tradition that keeps us honest. On a serious note the #noNUKESat SANO story is serious and we could do with some help to make some noise and put the brakes on storing nuclear waste at SanO. I'm back Saturday from the SUP retreat and would be happy to meet to discuss."

Joy floods my heart. Now here is an issue I can get behind. The San Onofre nuclear power generating station, just south of Trestles, had been pulled offline by the plant's owner, Southern

California Edison, when a 2012 steam generator leaked radiation. It has since been decommissioned, but 3.6 million pounds of nuclear waste are still on site and the current plan is for it to be buried there on the beach.

It is the stupidest thing I have ever heard—burying nuclear waste on a beach which also happens to be on a fault line, which also happens to be spitting distance from some twenty million people—but Southern California Edison is notoriously corrupt, as is California's Coastal Commission. It is mind-boggling that this is even a possibility, but it is, and this seems like the most fun fight ever.

I quickly message back, "Oh Ian... I love tossing barbs back and forth and it is so rare in our surf world for people not to take things so personally. Let's fuck So Cal Edison up. We should get Eddie Rothman involved!"

Eddie and Ian Cairns have a volatile history. The two have clashed for years, all beginning in 1975, when Australians first started competing in the North Shore surf contests and destroying the competition. Ian gave an interview to *Surfer* after winning the Duke Kahanamoku Invitational where he declared, "We're number one," referring to Australians as opposed to Hawaiians. He said, "We push ourselves harder than Hawaiians," and that North Shore locals had stagnated.

Fighting words don't come any more serious than those. Rothman had just cofounded Da Hui, a club of North Shore locals intent on not letting invading foreign hordes usurp Hawaiian resources anymore. They wore black shorts and slapped the shit out of anyone who looked at them sideways. And when Ian Cairns landed in the winter of 1976, Rothman and Da Hui were ready for him. There were death threats, teeth knocked out, threats of the Hawaiian mafia getting involved. Cairns spent a month locked in his hotel room before an uneasy peace was finally brokered by Eddie Aikau.

Da Hui still strikes fear into visiting surfers' hearts, and Eddie Rothman was re-infuriated about the whole situation when the documentary *Bustin' Down the Door* was released in 2009. It told the story of that 1976 winter, but Rothman didn't like it. "Bustin' down the door? There was no fuckin' door to bust down," he told me on his North Shore veranda with an angry growl. He was particularly angry that one of the movie's main characters, Rabbit Bartholomew, suggested that he had gotten beat up by a pack of Hawaiians at Sunset Beach. "You think it would take a group of us to beat him up? Ha. It would take maybe one. Maybe."

And my phone buzzes again. Ian has responded, "You hit on a huge idea. Enlist Eddie Rothman in the campaign. He's an environmentalist and what's halfway between Fukushima and Sano? Sunset Beach!"

Brilliant and is *this* it? Has *this* been my destiny all along? Cocaine led me to this moment right here, this bench. Cocaine brought me to myself. Surf journalism is going to save the world from nuclear waste, or at the very least southern California. Surf journalism, Ian Cairns, and Eddie Rothman. Now that is heroic.

I reach down, pull off one of my Reef's Mick Fanning beer bottle-opening sandals, grab the Stella patiently sitting next to me, and pop its cap. It's good. Refreshing. My mind is racing, plotting, building the story that will surely win awards. Maybe even a real Pulitzer? The characters are just too good. Better than I could ever create. The Bronzed Aussie and Fast Eddie? Eat your heart out, Elmore Leonard. My mind is racing so fast and so far that I don't even taste the usually unmistakable tang of dog shit, but I wouldn't have cared even if I had.

Surf journalism is going to save the world.

Timeline of Key Events

3000 BC • Peruvian fisherman surf the first waves ever.

3000 BC • Coca is gifted to Peruvians, and the world, by the gods.

0000-ish • Proto-Polynesians start surfing.

1499 • The explorer Amerigo Vespucci sees South Americans eating coca with "very ugly faces and expressions."

1769 • Captain James Cook observes surfing as he sails past Tahiti.

1855 • German chemist Friedrich Gaedcke isolates the specific cocaine alkaloid.

1872 • Mark Twain goes surfing in Hawaii.

1900 • Pure cocaine sells in the United States for twenty-five cents a gram.

1906 • Jack London discovers surfing and dubs it "The Sport of Kings."

1914 • The Harrison Narcotics Tax Act passes in the United States rendering the miracle drug illegal.

1927 • Sam Reid and Tom Blake surf Malibu for the very first time.

1932 • The first commercially produced surfboard goes on sale in California. It is called the "Swastika."

1947 • Thor Heyerdahl proves, beyond a shadow of a doubt, by sailing his Kon-Tiki that Peruvians took surfing to Polynesia.

1964 • The Endless Summer premieres.

1969 • Fred Hemmings pens "Pro Surfing is White" for *Surfer* magazine, defying drug use by surfers.

1974 • The G-Land surf camp opens in Grajagan, East Java.

1975 • David Bowie debuts his Thin White Duke and does so much cocaine that he sees angels coming to steal his semen.

1976 • Jeff Hakman travels to Australia with cocaine glassed in his fins, wins Bells, eats a doily, and gets US license for Quiksilver, giving proper birth to the surf industry.

1979 • Cocaine officially becomes Florida's largest import.

1979 • Michael Tomson founds Gotcha.

1982 • Ian Cairns founds the Association of Surfing Professionals.

1989 • Pablo Escobar makes it onto the Forbes billionaires list.

1990 • The professional surf tour organizers vote for drug testing but no tests are ever performed because the surfers insist the organizers must get tested too.

1994 • Chas Smith graduates high school and heads to Southern California into the belly of the cocaine and surfing beast.

1998 • Cocaine usage in Australia doubles.

2000 • The surf industry apocalypse begins in earnest.

2006 • Crack cocaine reaches its high water mark

2010 • Andy Irons dies of sudden cardiac in Texas with cocaine in his blood.

2018 • After brief talk, drug testing in professional surfing is more or less scuttled again it is business as usual for cocaine and surfing. To infinity and beyond!

Acknowledgments

I don't know if anyone really wants to be acknowledged in a book titled *Cocaine + Surfing*, but I can't not thank my gorgeous wife and two perfect daughters. My sun rises and sets with them. Or my fellow surf journalists. Or my agent, Dawn Frederick. Or the entire team at Rare Bird. Without all of you this book would never have existed. So...sorry*.

The apology does not extend to my fellow surf journalists who are all worthless bastards and deserve a book even worse than this one.

About the Author

CHAS SMITH is the author of *Welcome to Paradise, Now Go to Hell* (It Books / HarperCollins), which was optioned for television by Fox 21 (*Homeland* and *Sons of Anarchy*) with producers at Television 360 (*Game of Thrones*) and was a finalist for the PEN Center USA Award for Nonfiction. His latest title is *Reports From Hell* (Rare Bird, 2020), a memoir of his time spent in the Middle East in the early 2000s.

Chas began his writing career as a foreign correspondent, penning pieces for *Vice, Paper*, and *Blackbook*, amongst others, from Yemen, Lebanon, Syria, Somalia, Azerbaijan, and Colombia, which led to a brief career as a war correspondent for Current TV.

After being kidnapped by Hezbollah during the 2006 Israel-Lebanon war, he transitioned to surf journalism where he was a featured writer at the brash *Stab* before becoming editor at large at *Surfing Magazine*. There he developed a reputation as the most controversial voices in the space. Matt Warshaw, author of the *Encyclopedia of Surfing*, calls him, "Bright and hyper-ironic." He is the co-owner of a surf website, BeachGrit.